Canada Here We Come:

WITH THREE SUITCASES
AND A DAUGHTER

Steffie Steinke

Tellwell Talent
www.tellwell.ca

ISBN
978-0-2288-0642-4 (Paperback)
978-0-2288-0643-1 (eBook)

Table of Contents

Preface

We came to Canada on December 29, 1961.

By now many years have gone by and I (and so many others) realize that Canada has changed to the point where one wonders if we have lost our pride in being Canadians and take everything for granted this country has given us.

We all immigrated, some generations ago, some recently, but let's face it, immigrants made this country (and still do), but to what extent?

Especially, after World War II, in the 1950s and '60s, people came from other countries for many reasons; mostly, they wanted a better life.

There were no expectations or surprises when they made their first steps onto Canadian soil. It was clear to all that, after they received the proper papers and were approved for immigration, they were welcomed, but they were completely on their own.

People came here with the hope to make a better life for themselves, but they knew it would be without any help from the government other than to have the opportunity to get ahead and to live in peace.

Most immigrants made this country into what it is presently; they fulfilled their dreams by working hard and later became proud Canadians.

But some people wanted more; they wanted Canada to change to their liking, to their customs and religions.

It is a must to accept all people on an equal basis, but I believe, and so do many others that it's better not to ask Canada to change for you. Blend in and do what Canadians do. Be thankful that Canada

opened its doors and, with that, the opportunity to live here. It is not what you expect from Canada but, rather, what Canada expects from you.

Presently more and more people are sad and angry about the preferred privileges that have been made in order to please newcomers and wonder where it will end.

Canada spends millions of dollars to make life comfortable for whoever comes to this land. New immigrants have rights and freedoms as soon as they arrive. They are welcomed and are right away entitled to healthcare and social services. But many have complained that they are not looked after properly and blame it on discrimination.

The policy of multiculturalism is to encourage all to maintain their cultural traditions that are consistent with *Canadian values* (which are very tolerant already and should not be taken for granted).

Our laws should be changed, so it is clear to all, once immigrants choose to settle in Canada, they should blend in and do what is asked of them, to honour Canadian values, not values they once respected prior to coming to this land.

I read a very interesting article by Douglas Todd, in the *Vancouver Sun,* titled, "Immigration and the Welfare Dilemma," that provides another explanation as to why immigrants should be happy and should stop complaining about freedom and discrimination.

Canada is in many ways very generous to all, except, from my point of view, we forgot and neglected our poor and needy population, but presently concentrate more on immigration-related subjects. We should give priority to the poor and concentrate on eliminating this problem first before we give our unlimited attention to immigrants. Give the poor a job, not a small financial assistance where they can't live nor die on it. They too have a right to live a decent life!

For centuries, people came to Canada, and as I said, with only the hope and the will to make a better living here.

Many came alone, without their families or loved ones, but after they found work, they were a bit established and saw the future and opportunities Canada had to offer, they would ask their families to join them.

But to do so, they saved every dollar for a passage or flight, and again, it was not an easy task to receive proper immigration papers for their family members. They, too, had to go through the same process as other immigrants, and it took a lot of time before they were united with their families again.

We, my husband and our three-year-old daughter and I, came from Berlin, Germany with the hope of living in peace here. Germany was threatened by the Cold War, which was approaching with high speed.

A wall between East and West Germany was built so quickly that we became scared a new war would hit Europe again soon.

My husband heard about Canada and was seriously looking for a job, and, to my surprise, he found one. I, for many reasons, was not too sure but agreed to leave my homeland, with hesitation.

Since he had found a job, we thought it would be easy to get an immigration visa, but little did we know that it would not be easy at all.

There were many hurdles to overcome; we had to bring a ton of papers and had lengthy interviews at the Canadian embassy. They wanted a police report, plus health certificates from us and, later at the interview, we were told that we mustn't expect anything from the Canadian government at all.

We were also told, "Try to get work, learn English or French ASAP and integrate. If you want to practice your culture, then do so, but do it possibly at home, in church or in clubs, not so much in public."

Further, "Don't look down on people, rather, appreciate everybody. Once they, too, had relatives who went through the same experience as you will do when you arrive. Nobody is different in Canada; everyone is the same. Some are settled and some are not yet; some are Canadians, and some will become Canadians, but we are one proud nation and together we will grow. Should you not like these rules, don't criticize, but go back to where you came from."

It was a lot to understand, but well, we accepted all the rules full-heartedly and with a lot of hope. It was hard, but we thought we would learn quickly.

The worse thing was that I didn't speak English at all, my husband only a little and my daughter didn't care; all she wanted was to go back home.

At the time we came, Canada had no social securities but very affordable private insurance. Some people were insured by the company they worked for, some paid for their own private insurance, and most people were OK with that. Nobody complained. To us, it was suggested that we should buy health insurance before going to Canada, and so we did. (We learned a bit later that it was a good suggestion.)

But that was then

The country grew with the help of the people and a government that planned for a future for everybody.

Soon, some social systems were introduced and, after, people who worked for a certain time in Canada were entitled to receive these benefits. A huge step forward!

The middle class bloomed and, as I remember, everybody's dream was to own a house.

Canada's economy was getting better, and many people earned a decent salary and were able to fulfill their dreams.

We bought our first house in 1965. It was the biggest investment we had ever made, and a dream, which became true and that we never could have fulfilled in the old country.

But, as I said, that was then and isn't anymore. I guess we widened our "views" to make this country special!

A country where new immigrants don't ask but demand, and where apologies are made for mistakes going back to almost the first settlers, and instead of learning from mistakes, we continue to promise but don't follow up. The next government is voted in, promises are made but not fulfilled and, guess what, we apologize again. An endless, expensive chain.

Nowadays, monuments are destroyed because people don't want to be reminded of what was done wrong in the past and learn from it to do better in the future; they would rather remove the wrongdoing completely.

History should be a lesson to make changes for the better if something was done wrong. We try, but we would rather apologize and pay for each apology! It is a good way out.

As I mentioned before, we should learn from mistakes, instead of constantly apologizing for wrongdoings, which were done, most of the time, decades and centuries ago.

Still, the question remains: are we catering to new immigrants more than we do to the people who came earlier, who came without any rights except to immigrate and be welcomed to this country? I strongly think we do!

Our government apologizes and pays for the smallest complaint as soon as the Charter of Rights and Freedoms is mentioned!

And I asked, why don't people go back to their country if they don't like it in our country?

Canada gives to all of us a good life, a life many never had in their homeland. So, instead of being thankful, some bring up their rights, get heard, and at times get millions of dollars, if our government sees a reason or wants to avoid legal actions. (Example: Omar Khadr settlement suing the Canadian government, article by Maham Abedi, Global News, July 4, 2017)

People have worked hard to make this country attractive, and Canada has become a favoured destination to begin a new life. Yet so many who have come over without many rights or expectations don't understand and often shake their heads about the changes that have been made to give new immigrants rights that ordinary people wouldn't even dream of having, and now, in many people's view, Canada is not one country but increasingly a place where everybody singles themselves out instead of blending in.

Changes have gone too far, not only the changes made to please immigrants, but to many other people. We have even changed our national anthem and made it gender-neutral.

And again, where is our national pride? It has disappeared! We make changes to be politically correct according to everybody's wishes and complaints. (See article by Paul Tasker, CBC News, Dreams of gender-neutral O Canada are over-for now)

When we arrived, we came to a mostly Christian land. Unfortunately, now we mustn't say Merry Christmas any longer, but should, to please other people's religions, say "Happy Holidays." (Refer to the blog from Christopher Taylor, "If We Can't Say 'Merry Christmas' in Canada, Multiculturalism Failed")

Christians can't pray in school or public places because it might offend people of other religions; yet, pupils of another religion can say their prayers, and if they do so can request special rooms. (See article by Dan Levin, *The New York Times;* "A Battle over Prayer in Schools Tests Canada's Multiculturalism")

As mentioned, we had no help from the government when we arrived, but now new immigrants for example receive paid living expenses, including rent (paid with our taxes).

Immigrants who received their Canadian citizenship wearing a niqab or burka to cover up their faces, as I understand, had a legal challenge and after, are allowed to continue do so.

Canadian dignitaries, ministers, and people in public services represent our country covering up their hair, by wearing turbans or shawls out of cultural or religious reasons.

(And the question remains, if Christians can't say "Merry Christmas" any longer, the government and public institutions, in general, should stay out of all, be it religious or cultural reasons and should have a dress code accordingly; in western style, depending on the occasion, business-like or casually.)

We are not a country anymore where "one" does what Canadians do. We have become a country where immigrants tell us what their rights are and will prove it by suing Canada if they are not respected. And in a way I can't blame them, it's our government's fault; they created the dilemma.

Older generations helped and worked very hard to make this beautiful land what it has become, strong and proud, but I and many others believe that doesn't count any longer.

Instead of focusing on immigrants, the government must increase and focus on making it better for the poor people in our country. People live on streets in heat or cold, with very little or nothing to eat or to care for their families.

So, what about looking after hunger and homelessness, the poor or the old people first?

When I bring these subjects up, most of the time I hear, "We try, but don't have the money to help everybody at the same time."

As you realize, I, and so many others, are not impressed and are actually sad!

And yes, maybe my voice doesn't count much nowadays, but what I can tell you is my story, our beginning in Canada, and the hope I have is that the people will come to a solution where we all will blend-in and become "ONE," where Canadians do again what Canadians did long before the new wave of immigrants came to Canada, regardless of colour, creed or religion but choose to stay and integrate without asking for extras or preferred treatments. I am afraid that if we don't do that, Canada will lose its identity soon.

So it is understandable that many people are not too happy about the pronounced diversity we have going on, but prefer that we go back to the old understanding where everybody who is a Canadian or will become a Canadian is proud to be one without special treatments.

Nobody, at the time we came, took it as a right to be here, but as a privilege to live in this country where freedom and pride are priorities. Canada opened its doors for us all, to give us opportunities for a better life. We must be thankful.

Immigrants who are willing to blend-in and don't pressure us to adapt to them will help to unite all of us to be "One Canada" again.

Berlin, Germany 1957 to 1961

We lived in West Berlin, close to the border of East Berlin, and life was good but so different from East Berlin. The East side had beautiful landscapes, and often, on weekends, we went over to the East side for walks or to visit relatives. Our little daughter Sabrina loved these outings and we, too, looked forward to having the time together.

The summer of 1961 was wonderful; it was warm and sunny and yet not too hot, just right for walks and little trips. So, yes, since we both worked and Sabrina was during the week with my foster-mother who babysat, weekends were special.

Towards the middle of July, we heard rumours that East Berliners were restless and that many had left or planned to leave the East to settle in West Germany or in West Berlin.

We didn't really see anything wrong with that since West Berlin's future was bright, many had good jobs. The difference between East and West was like day and night. For instance, the reconstruction on the East side was very slow, hardly visible, and the stores were mostly empty. Groceries and other goods were hard to get. The West side, on the contrary, had no shortages whatsoever except living space. To have your own apartment was a dream and many people were lucky if they found a room to rent.

Since Berlin was mostly in ruins, Dietmar and I were lucky because shortly before we married, we had found a nice room on a very quiet street with a view of a park.

Our happiness was complete, especially after we told my foster-mother that we had found a room, and she offered to buy the furniture for it.

As she told us, "This is your wedding present from me, but you can choose between me paying for the wedding or for the furniture. I can't pay for both."

We chose the furniture and thought we had won the lottery. At least, I felt like that. I wasn't too sure about Dietmar, but when I asked him about it, he assured me that I shouldn't worry. He was as happy as I was.

Dietmar came from a very well-off family who lived in a wonderful house with many rooms and bathrooms etc.

His father owned a very successful textile business and bought the house shortly after the war ended. They had the house completely renovated, and for me, it was like a castle.

When Dietmar introduced me to his parents, I was not very welcomed since his parents, as Dietmar told me, had another girl in mind for him, and, in their eyes, I was too poor. But, he couldn't have cared less, and after almost three years of dating, we got engaged in May 1956 and married in 1957.

After we told Dietmar's parents about our wedding plans, they offered to have us live with them in Dietmar's room, but we declined; we wanted to be on our own and would make do with what we had.

So, yes, Dietmar had to change his lifestyle from, at that time, a rich environment to a very simple life without his own room or maid, but he didn't blink when we signed the lease for the little room we had found. And when I asked him again if he was sure about changing to having only one room, with the bathroom and a kitchen we had to share with the owner's family, he assured me that he was happy and said, "I love you, and one day we will make it, and we will be proud that we started with nothing. You will see," and I believed him.

I, myself, came from a poor home. My foster-mother Meta Pech, whom we called *Muttchen*, worked long hours cleaning apartment buildings and other people's apartments and houses to make ends meet, but we never complained, especially after what we all had to experience during and after the war.

After our wedding, we moved into that little rented room and stayed there for almost nine months.

We tried to get our own apartment, but the waiting list was too long, and there was no hope that we would ever get an apartment. Even

so, it was hopeless; we waited, but without success. We were happy; we both had a job and had each other.

But one day, my mother-in-law, Else, called me at work (like most people, we had no phone at home) to tell me that we might get a small apartment. She explained that the apartment building was brand new, built by friends of my in-laws and they could, as per government rules, keep one bachelor apartment for themselves, and since they had no intention of moving in, they would be happy to rent it to us.

Oh, how good was that of them to think about us?

I said to Dietmar's mother without even seeing the apartment, "Yes." But later when we saw it, we found it perfect for the two of us. Imagine having an apartment all for ourselves!

A combination of a living room/dining room/bedroom with a kitchenette, a little hall and a bathroom with a tub and warm and cold water. What a luxury! The apartment was on the first floor and had a very large window in the living area, and even a window in the small kitchen. We were ecstatic; it was small but simply cute, and our furniture would fit into it too. We couldn't believe our luck.

The building was on Forster Strasse in Kreuzberg, not in the best district of Berlin, but who cared!

We moved to our brand-new apartment on December 31, 1957 and didn't unpack much because we had been invited by my in-laws to celebrate New Year's Eve with them and their many friends. I was always so amazed at how many people they invited. It was a great party, a lot of fun, and Dietmar and I were very happy.

As I mentioned, we both worked and had little, but we could pay our bills and, for us, that was wonderful and the most important thing.

A month or so later, after the New Year's party, I became violently sick, and we thought I had the flu, but no, I was pregnant. This was a surprise, but we were happy, and a baby would be very much welcomed. We hadn't planned on having a baby yet, but so what, we had an apartment and didn't have to cope with one room, without our own bathroom and kitchen. Imagining that we had our own bathroom—the thought of it always made us happy.

We didn't tell anybody about my pregnancy right away, but after being pregnant for eight weeks with the vomiting not stopping, rather, it became worse, we had to.

When Dietmar told our parents about it, they were pleased, but both my foster-mother and Dietmar's mother told me that I must see a doctor at once. I didn't think it was necessary yet because I thought, what could he do? And in the times we lived, you didn't go to the doctor until you showed or unless you were sick and didn't feel well, and boy, was I sick! So, so sick that I thought something was wrong, and I became scared.

One morning, Dietmar had had enough and called the doctor, using a phone from his work, to tell him all the details and that he was worried. Our doctor came within the hour to our apartment, but by the time he arrived, I was so weak that I wasn't able to open the door. I had fainted behind it. The doctor heard the noise and must have called on our neighbour because when I became conscious again, I heard him talking to somebody. Aware that I must have fainted, I told him that the door was unlocked, but I couldn't get up. He, with the help of the neighbour, came in, almost stepping on me, and both helped me to get up, taking me to the bed.

The neighbour stayed in the kitchen while our doctor examined me and assured me that I was pregnant but that he was very upset that I hadn't seen him sooner. He asked my neighbour to call for an ambulance saying, "Tell them to hurry, she is completely dehydrated and needs help fast."

I was put on intravenous at once, and stayed on intravenous for, on and off, three months because whenever they tried to take me off it, I started to vomit again. I lost ten pounds and looked awful. When I could finally go home, I couldn't believe that I was still alive and wondered how our baby was doing but was assured that the baby was fine; it was me they were worried about.

Even so, I lost all that weight, I started to show, and when I went to see the doctor again, he confirmed that the baby was fine. I was so happy, and we all looked forward to having our baby in our lives.

It was a difficult, hard pregnancy. I didn't stop vomiting until I gave birth, but I was coping, and after 27 hours of labour, Sabrina was born in October 1958, and in our eyes, she was the cutest, good-looking baby on earth. She was so perfect and looked like a doll. Her little face was surrounded by thick black hair. As a matter of fact, for the first week or so, she was covered with fine black hair all over her little body, and we thought we had a little monkey. I was assured that some babies

were born with body hair, but again, not to worry, it will disappear. She had beautiful big eyes, surrounded by long, black eyelashes, and everybody who saw her wanted to pick her up and cuddle her, but both Dietmar and I were very protective.

Soon after we brought her home, we realized that Sabrina was a very nervous baby and cried a lot. Any noise would wake her up, and she would scream for hours. Our lives changed dramatically.

I tried to nurse her, but she didn't drink much and would vomit constantly, and my foster-mother said, "She is colicky, stop nursing. She maybe isn't taking your milk well or doesn't like your milk." (Nice compliment.)

And our doctor agreed and suggested that I should pump and give her my milk in a bottle, or change to formula since he, too, believed that she wasn't getting enough and maybe cried because she was hungry.

So, I started to pump. At the time, the German government paid 50 Pfennig daily for nursing and, to us, it was a lot of help, and so I stretched out the pumping as long as I could.

To get this money every two weeks, I had to see my doctor who then had to verify that I still had milk.

Yet, whatever the reason was, the new method didn't help for long. Biena still vomited my milk out until I started to change to formula, which she kept in. Perhaps my foster-mother was right; she didn't like my milk also any noise. She didn't sleep much, and if we made the slightest noise, she screamed from the top of her lungs.

Dietmar worked shifts and when he was on night shift, I would go to my foster-mother for much of the day, so he could sleep.

Surprisingly, when I gave her the bottle and put her in the noise-less bedroom, she slept without a problem.

I told Dietmar about it, and we realized that our small bachelor apartment was fine for us, but we needed a separate bedroom. Our daughter needed quiet surroundings; she couldn't take the noise.

We started looking for something suitable but couldn't find anything for the longest time.

One weekend, Dietmar pointed out an advertisement to me, where a single lady wanted to exchange her one-bedroom apartment into something closer to her children, actually right where we lived than. The apartment was located in Neukoelln, Weder Str.

We went to have a look, but it wasn't like what we had presently; it had no bathroom, only a toilet without a tub, no warm water, and the oven only heated the bedroom and living room. Both kitchen and bathroom had no heating whatsoever. On the other hand, we had a nice-sized kitchen, a living room, and a large bedroom. It was an old building, which survived the war. At one point, it must have had gas lighting, we could see the old connections and that it had been changed over to electricity. The wires were outside the walls and had to be correctly installed.

We didn't commit, but after she asked us about our apartment and what we had to offer, the old woman was keen to see it as soon as possible. We promised we would let her know.

When we returned home, I told Dietmar that this was not what I had hoped for, and it was a "no" from me. Dietmar thought differently about it, and said with his charming smile, a smile I never could resist, "It has potential, and, yes, we must renovate, and must have a water heater installed in the kitchen etc., and we have to go to your foster-mother's for a bath, but look at it this way, the rent is less than what we pay presently, so we will have a bit of money left over. And the main thing is, we will have so much additional room and, hopefully, the baby will sleep better."

He painted a picture that made the old apartment look like a castle and won me over, and so I sat down and looked at our household finances and made a budget to make sure we could afford the move.

This renovation project would not only take the little bit of the savings we had, it would put us into the red. For me, this alone made a simple "no," but for Dietmar, it was "Oh, we will manage."

I had a little book where, when we paid our rent, we got a stamp from the landlord for each month after the payment was made.

At that time we only dealt with cash; so we didn't know how to pay things by cheque. We hardly knew about bank accounts, and in order not to overspend, I used each empty page in our "rent book" for putting money aside for anything we needed during the month. It was my little budget. Any money left over would go into a jar and was our rescue, in case we needed something out of the ordinary.

In doing all that, I realized that I should go back to work. With Dietmar's salary, we managed only from month to month and with

Sabrina, not a year old yet, there were a lot of expenses we hadn't included in our budget. So again, with all the renovations Dietmar talked about, we would be in the hole.

Dietmar didn't want me to go back to work, but I explained it would be better, and my foster-mother could babysit.

He looked at me. "So, you talked already to *Muttchen* about going back to work?"

"Yes, I did. I think it would be good, but with the move, it would be necessary. I will check if my old company has a position open for me and if so, we could plan. Otherwise, I will have to look for a different job and that could take time since there are not very many jobs to choose from anymore."

At the time I had Sabrina, the maternity leave in Germany was six weeks before and six weeks after the baby was born. So, it could be that there was no opening for me.

I phoned my old company and was asked to come in the next morning.

It would be great to work there again. I liked my job and the people I worked with.

The interview was quick. I was told that I could start the next week and would get my old job back with an increase in my salary. What a joy!

There was one problem. At the moment, from the location where we lived, the way to take Sabrina to my foster-mother would not be too far, but after our move, it would be very difficult. I hoped I could manage.

We moved two months later to the new location and, I must say, my husband and some other hired workers made a nice renovation job; the apartment became a comfortable and nice place to live in. We borrowed some money from my foster-mother and made sure we were able to pay it back soon.

I had to work out a timetable as to how to get on time to work but was at first not sure how to manage it. I had to be at the office at 7:00 A.M., but I had to take Sabrina first to my foster-mother, which took a half hour one way and was in the opposite direction, and I had to consider practically two hours to get punctually to work.

I woke Sabrina at 4:30 A.M., which was hard at first on both of us, and I thought that this would not work out, but after the second day I had it under control and figured out a time frame that was better and worked out fine. I took the subway at 5:15 A.M., and we arrived at my foster-mother's at a quarter to six. *Muttchen* took the baby out of the carriage and put her straight into her bed, where Sabrina, most of the time, slept until 8 A.M.

After a week, the routine was working and since Sabrina loved my foster-mother, she wasn't crying anymore when I left her, and I knew she was in good hands. Mind you, when I picked her up by about 4:30 in the afternoon, she had been spoiled rotten and wanted to stay.

We paid off our debts to my foster-mother punctually as promised and for that, she gave us money to buy an old Volkswagen. Our first car. Two days later, the night before we picked up the car, we both couldn't sleep. We were so excited, and thought we were rich.

The thing was so old that when it rained, we had to stop to clean the windows because the wipers didn't work. We had no money to have it fixed, but we made out fine. We didn't complain. We coped with many issues that old car had, and yet for us it was great, and we made do. We were happy.

Later, when we both had a raise, we bought a better car, but during the week we took public transportation because it was a bit cheaper.

My *Muttchen* was our angel; she helped us wherever she could. Even so, she had not really an income other than her little pension from the government, she saved every penny she could for us. We borrowed, we paid back and borrowed again. She was our bank, and she taught us how to handle money.

Sabrina was growing up quickly and became cuter all the time. She spoke very well for her age and made us laugh many times. She was two and a half and wanted an explanation for every new word she heard.

We had to watch ourselves, not to speak the "Berliner Slang" since we wanted her to speak "Hoch Deutsch" (High German) or as we were told in school, the "correct German." But when we sometimes had a slang word in our vocabulary, she promptly corrected us often and would say, "You said the word wrong." It became a game for her, but for us, it was funny since she still had a lot of baby language in her vocabulary and we had to make sure she didn't see us laughing at her. She tried so hard to be correct, in order to correct us. We learned to take her very seriously. She had fun and played with us quite often. She would carry on until we admitted to her that the word we just said was wrong and that we shouldn't talk like that.

The good thing about it was, she learned very quickly to speak correctly. If she couldn't sound out a word or sentence properly and if it sounded funny, we just repeated it correctly, and she would say with a very straight face, "Yes, that is right, and I will remember!"

She gave us so much joy, and we had to watch that we, including my foster-mother, didn't spoil her too much. The same with my in-laws. My father-in-law couldn't resist her at all, and she knew it. He, who was so serious and proper, was the worst in allowing her almost anything. Sabrina could never do wrong. We were sometimes angry with him, but, we were never heard. He always would say, "Just let it go, who knows how long we can spoil her?" And he was right because at that time we didn't have the slightest idea that it was good that she was spoiled by her loved ones, since soon we would realize how everything can change in a very short time, almost overnight.

What were the Russians planning?

It was not too long after the conversation with my father-in-law that we learned that our homeland was in danger again. Already in July, East Berliners had trouble crossing the borders to the West side, and it made many people nervous. The controls started to become stricter including all allied personnel and military officials, who normally could enter all sectors freely and without restrictions, they only had to show their passports, regardless if they were in or without their uniforms.

When Khrushchev, in a speech, warned that a military build-up would be necessary to stop the migration from the East to the West, panic broke out. The amount of people leaving the East blocks was becoming overwhelming and many left their homes without their belongings. They walked away and tried to escape to the West sector. Some hoped that they would be able to come back after the West stepped in, but no, there was no interference from the Allies at all.

The flow of people leaving was upsetting for the East side since they lost too many people and with that, also their workforce. So, they had to change their policy. And they did. Controls, which were usually done by both Russian military and East German soldiers, were suddenly handled by East German soldiers only, and since allied personal never had to answer to Germans before, trouble was brewing at once.

Germans on both sides became nervous and by mid-summer, an increasing number of people from the East were leaving, fleeing to the West.

Rumours had it that the East would close its borders soon for good, and by mid-July, thousands of refugees had arrived in West Berlin, escaping from the communist regime of East Germany.

Many people thought that such a tragedy could never happen and stayed put, and those who left hoped to return soon back to their homes. Nobody could believe that a country could be separated. But they were wrong.

Real panic set in on August 13, 1961: East Germany closed the East-West border and the Soviet military encircled the city to endorse the closing.

When we heard on the news what had happened, we became scared and thought that we would be encountering a new war.

I, in particular, was very nervous since a few years before, my birth mother and I returned from Poland where we were captured after the war. The memory was too fresh, and I never wanted to live through all of that again.

Thousands had left their homes, and the stream of people was endless. They arrived in West Berlin and the West took them all. Camps were opened and help was provided. Many were taken in by relatives, but most people were referred to West Germany directly, where refugees became a burden. The government simply was not prepared for the invasion of so many people and had no space nor camps in place to take them in. And yet, everybody wanted to help, and nobody gave up. They tried to cope and did until escape was no longer possible. Most borders were closed, a wall was built, and the few crossovers left open were almost impossible to pass.

Even under normal circumstances, to cross the border was always a nerve-wracking experience and not pleasant. Border guards at best were very strict and never friendly, and if they detected anything suspicious, people had to come up with a good reason or had to show a special visa. But regardless, they had always to explain in details why they wanted to cross the borders.

As we had heard, it was very risky because if the East guards had the slightest reason to stop you from entering the west sector, they would send you to jail at once. The controls were strict, and it made it almost impossible to enter the West side.

They closed eighty open crossings and reduced them to seven, which were guarded by heavily armed East German soldiers and made it unbelievably hard to even find a good reason to cross. Ordinary passports were not acceptable, and West Berliners had to pay in West Marks if they wanted to visit somebody in the East.

On August 26, Soviet tanks moved into East Berlin to face off with U.S. tanks on the West side. By Thursday, August 31, 1961, the Berlin Wall was hastily and speedily installed, first with a two-foot-high barbed-wire fence and a bit later with prefabricated, 11.8 foot high blocks of concrete that made it clear that this had been planned beforehand. From one day to the next, East Germany was completely divided by an altogether 111.9 km long wall from West Germany. It was installed so quickly that people could hardly comprehend what had happened. A very difficult situation to believe.

We visited the border on Saturday and couldn't understand what happened and what we saw. We realized that it was true what we had heard on the news.

In our area, the wall was still low, marked with barbed wire, and when we were close enough, our daughter let go of my hand and ran towards it to jump over it. She thought we would continue our walk. I yelled and called her back, but she continued to run and shortly before she tried to jump, a VOPO (East police officer) called over to us to take the child and walk away. He was friendly and apologetic, but we knew he meant it. My husband called Sabrina again, and this time she listened. She asked why she couldn't go there, and my husband, after he had grabbed her hand, explained that the police officer didn't want us going any further. She asked why again, but Dietmar didn't say anything, only came quickly to me and said, "Come home. This is too much for me to comprehend. These poor people over on the other side must be devastated. And our relatives, will we be able to see them again?" He was very upset and angry.

We rushed home, and there I had a fit. All my memories came back, and I wanted to run. I cried and couldn't stop, and Dietmar was helpless. He realized the terrible times I had to endure during and after the war came back to me. He hugged me and said, "I am sure this will soon come to an end, and the Allies will not allow this nonsense."

But I cried on and answered, "And it will end with a war again, you will see. Oh God, I never thought it could happen again."

Germany is divided

Everybody was shocked and frightened, but some left, even so, they risked their lives because they were shot at. It was confusing and yet real, so very real. Germans were shooting at Germans.

O, my God! Not long ago World War II had ended, then came the blockade, and now the division between East and West Germany. What might be next? A war again? Why? Everybody was asking what was wrong with this world. Nobody understood.

When I came the next day to work, one-third of my colleagues were gone; they were not able to come to work because of the division between East and West.

We were all shocked, and it was so unbelievable. Many colleagues had worked there since the end of the war. We couldn't even say a proper goodbye to them. The situation was so sad because it came practically overnight that we lost all contact with them. The telephone lines were cut, and there was no communication between the East and West at all. No mail service, and no telephone service, nothing whatsoever.

Everything was so, so sad and nobody could understand the change in such a short time.

Berliners were tough because of the war, but again? It was too much to cope with, and most asked themselves constantly why? But the answers were simple; most Germans disagreed with the communist regime; the politics didn't agree with the freedom the Germans wanted and dreamed of. They had had enough from dictatorships, and with that, many people left their homes to establish a life in West Germany. The result was that the East side had no workers any longer and their economy collapsed completely. At my work, approximately forty per cent lived in East Berlin. They were paid in West Mark and since the exchange rate was 1.00 East Mark for 0.45 Pfennig in Deutsche Mark they made good money. East Berliners wouldn't give up their jobs in West Berlin for anything. West Berlin's economy was booming, and East Berliners had no problem finding a job in the West, and even if they made less money there, the exchange rate made up for it. It was much higher than they would have made in East Germany. So again, East Berlin ran out of manpower, and the solution was either get rid of the borders or close them completely.

The division was brutal but had been planned for a while; the wall was built in only a few weeks and was there to stay.

We are thinking of moving

Dietmar and I were very upset, probably because we lived so close to the border and the Allies didn't do anything but stand on the West side. Pointing their cannons towards the East side didn't help.

As we had heard, there were negations in progress, but without success, the East refused to give in. As a matter of fact, negotiations were broken off, and East border guards were even increasing the number of their soldiers.

Many people didn't give up and tried to make it over to the West side, but most were caught and punished. The system worked; it was an unforgiveable one.

Dietmar had talked about moving to West Germany, but I was not ready to do that because, even so, I was very nervous and Dietmar told me that I was having nightmares again. I didn't want to move.

Due to the immigrants coming from the East, jobs in West Germany and in Berlin were recently hard to come by. There were too many refugees who gladly took any job. As a matter of fact, the unemployment figures were unimaginable, and salaries were going down. So, if one had work, one stayed put and didn't complain.

I didn't want to live somewhere else, and when he came up with the idea to go, I thought he had made a bad joke, but no, he talked increasingly about it, and I realized he meant it.

I told Dietmar to wait; I was sure it would end, and the East would negotiate with the West, and they will make amends.

I didn't want to give in to letting my memories play tricks on me. I thought, the situation will go away. After all, we lived on the West side, we both had good jobs, and our daughter was happy to stay with my foster-mother during the day. So, what else could we want?

Notwithstanding, as time went by, we realized that it wasn't the same; we felt the tension, and we still thought it will end up with war.

Life went on without the hope that the East would ever open the borders again and the wall between us grew. The Allies didn't do a thing. Yes, they protested; they marched in and out of the zones to show their rights, but nothing else. It was a power game.

The wall was there to stay, and we thought we should move. Who knows what would come next? Many people talked about war. There was hardly a conversation without using the word, and it was uncomfortable to live under that kind of pressure.

I talked about Dietmar's thoughts to my foster-mother at length, but she just answered, "He is, in one way, right; our situation is serious and if you go, I will miss you all." She almost cried, but continued, "You go where your husband goes; I trust him, and he will do the right thing for you and Sabrina. So, where would you go?"

I looked at her. "I don't know."

I was surprised when she said, "You will figure it out." She didn't object to us moving, but maybe she was right; she was always right.

One day, in the beginning of September, Dietmar came home from work and asked me if I would go to Canada. He was offered a job there and could start as soon as we had all the papers together.

"Canada? Where is that? Is that not close to America, over the ocean?" I asked in shock.

"Yes, Canada! But so what? We could have a new beginning, and you wouldn't to have to work; you would be able to stay home with Sabrina. I understand the money I will make will be sufficient to feed a family."

I looked at him. I couldn't understand what he was talking about. After some silence, I asked him how much he would make, and Dietmar, I guess, not so sure of himself right then, looked at me and said, "I don't have a figure yet."

"Do they pay for the flight over because we have to fly, right? And that would be very expensive." His answer was no. "We would have to pay for the flight ourselves, but I think we will make it there just fine."

I couldn't understand my husband at that point and was so puzzled and told him plain and simple that I thought he was nuts. I was

very upset about the whole thing. We didn't talk that evening for quite a while, but I started by saying, "I don't understand you, Dietmar. You have no clue how much you will make; they won't pay for the flight and you still think it is a good deal?"

We had our first major fight.

I thought about my foster-mother and my mother. Yes, I wasn't close to my mother, but she was after all my mother, and how about Dietmar's family, what would they say?

No, I was surely not prepared to go that far away. And what would become of all our belongings? Could we take that with us? No was the answer. We had to sell all, but we would buy new stuff over there. In Dietmar's eyes, everything would work out. He wanted to go so badly and I didn't understand how fast he was prepared to leave everything behind.

He could speak a bit of English; he used to play with American kids, but I couldn't. I just had a bit of school English, taught by an old German teacher who, I was sure, didn't speak so well either. So, how could I understand my surroundings if I could hardly understand what people were talking about? Just the thought was awful. And Sabrina (we all called her Biena, except my mother-in-law who called her Bienlein), how would she cope? All these questions without any answers.

We talked to both our families and heard different opinions. My mother thought we were out of our minds. My foster-mother, once again, was on Dietmar's side. She thought that, at this point, we might be better off if we went. And my in-laws were in shock and thought, we both lost it, but later, in principle were not against it too much or didn't want to say anything.

So, what to do? The only reason I would agree to all of that was if I didn't have to work and could stay home with Biena. Dietmar was so excited about it all that nothing could stop him.

He told me, "We could always come back."

"To what?" I asked. I was so confused. I didn't know what to say at all and was thinking, was this my Dietmar I married?

We didn't have that much time to make up our minds. As Dietmar explained to me, McGregor Hosiery, the name of the company, was very interested in having him soon and would help to speed up the process of receiving the visa by getting in contact with the Canadian embassy.

Dietmar jumped after he received the message, and I cried; everything was too quick. I certainly was not yet prepared for it at all.

The next day, I talked to a girl at work about my dilemma. She, right away, thought this was a wonderful opportunity and said if she were me, she wouldn't think about it twice, especially at the time we lived in right then. I only looked at her and told her that I had my doubts. And further, I said, "What should we do with all the furniture and our apartment?"

"Now with that, I might be able to help," she said, "because I know a couple who is desperately looking for an apartment. They are getting married next month and will live with his parents until they find something suitable. I will ask them and let you know by tomorrow."

I didn't mention anything to Dietmar about my conversation because it was so hard even to think about leaving most of our belongings behind us.

Next morning, my colleague came back to me and told me that her friends were very interested, and I should let her know when they could see the apartment.

For me, all this couldn't be true; it was a bad dream. I thought we should stay and yet, I didn't have the nerve to tell Dietmar.

If my foster-mother would have just said to me that this was all wrong, I would have at least protested, but no, everybody thought this was a good thing. After all, it was a few years after World War II, and then the blockade, and now the wall. Oh yes, for Germany, Canada, and the USA had their streets plastered with gold. How could one not go if the opportunity called for it?

Eventually, I told Dietmar that, maybe, I had found somebody who could take or buy our apartment, including the furniture. He was ecstatic and asked, "So, you will go?"

And my answer was, "Not really, but I…yes, I will."

It was time to get our house in order. We had to sell our little car, a Fiat, which we just bought recently. By the way, the car was the first thing we bought and paid with monthly payments, rather than in full.

We practically had to sell everything that we couldn't put in a suitcase, and since we had no money to ship anything over by boat, we lost a lot.

Dietmar had no problems with any of it; he wanted to go, and he was fulfilling his dream going over to America or in our case to Canada.

In another three weeks, we received a letter from the Canadian embassy to advise us that we were invited for an interview and should let them know if the time they gave us was suitable for us. We had to bring a police report and a health history with us, which we already had by then. We realized the whole adventure was becoming a reality and we had to say "yes or no," and in the end, we both said "YES."

The interview went fine and even our three-year-old daughter behaved. After a while, she asked why we had to be in this room but before we could answer, she was told by the very friendly gentleman who interviewed us that she will be going on a big trip, and said to her, "I am sure you will like it." But, she was not very pleased about the possibility of going on a trip and wanted to cry, saying that she didn't want to go unless we went too. Dietmar laughed and assured her that we never would leave her. She looked at us and saw that we meant it and became so excited about it that we forget our worries because our daughter liked the idea too.

Soon after talking about all the paperwork and thinking we were finished, we got up from our seats, and the gentleman said, "Oh, before we part, I just want to give you some advice, of course, if you don't mind. I am sure that you will receive the visa within two or three weeks because your employer mentioned that you are needed in Canada since not many people are skilled enough to work for them in the position you are wanted for. But, if you want to make Canada your home, I would like to suggest that you try to blend in by learning English first and do like the Canadians do. The government will not help you; you are on your own, and there is no social security at all. Maybe the company you will work for has a private health insurance, but for the first 3 to 4 months, you have to have your own insurance. The best thing is, you arrange that from here because you never know when you need it. I wish you luck and success!"

He got up, and we shook hands and left the room. In the hall, we hugged and cried and Biena didn't know what to think about it but didn't say a word.

On our way back home, we didn't talk at all; we just looked blank. I didn't know how we made it home.

Arriving home, I walked around, pointing at the furniture.

"This all has to go! We have to sell everything and fast because we have practically only six weeks before we have to leave. I don't know how to do it, do you?"

Dietmar looked at me and answered, "No, but didn't you have somebody at work? You mentioned something like that the other day. You said that they would like to buy the whole apartment as is and would pay cash."

"Yes, I did, but they want to look at the apartment first. I will let the girl know tomorrow because she is very anxious to let her friend know about our decision."

I couldn't understand how cool Die was about all of this, and how quickly he was able to part from everything we had. But again, I thought, he sees his dream fulfilled, going to Canada, yet I follow him because I love him.

At one time, long before we knew each other, he wanted to go to the States. He had an uncle living there, but it fell through before it started. He told me that his uncle didn't want to sponsor him because Dietmar had just finished high school and was told by his uncle that he should attend college or something first.

His uncle was vice-president for the international marketing department at Wrigley's. I met him in Germany when he and his wife visited the family in Berlin. I liked them both very much. But at the time I met them, we were engaged and very happy and Dietmar didn't even think of going to the States, and little did I know that he would have loved going to America and that explained why he never lost that urge and now would be able to fulfill his dream.

The next day, I mentioned to my colleague again at work that our plans to leave Berlin had become serious and asked if her friends were still interested in buying the apartment including furniture and taking over our lease. She said, "I know they are, but I'll let them know."

They came on the weekend to view our apartment and were ecstatic about it. As we realized later, we quoted them too low a price, and everything was sold in a second, and after they left, we both cried. I remember only that I hoped our landlord would refuse the change to sublease our apartment, but he didn't, and, therefore, in about four

weeks, we would be without anything, except what we could get into three suitcases and three big carry-ons, depending on the weight. We had no money nor an address to have anything sent over by boat, and we for sure didn't have the nerves to ask anybody to help us.

Again, Dietmar was so full of hope and just said, "Don't worry, we will make it." I had no other choice than to believe him that he was right.

I quit my job with two weeks' notice and had another week before we were leaving Germany. My job, another thing I had to leave behind. I was sad because I loved the job and the people there.

We bought a few things for the trip, like three big suitcases and hand luggage, and for Sabrina, everything new because she grew again, and it was not worthwhile to take her old clothes with us. She was very happy about it; she loved clothes, and it took her mind off asking constantly why I was crying and packing stuff.

Dietmar worked until December 23 and took the car back to the dealership we had bought it from. It was like brand new, but after he returned, he was not unhappy. I was sure he didn't realize what went on at home since he thought that that was my responsibility.

I started seriously packing the week after I left my job. Every day I got another suitcase packed, except the bedding, which I stuffed into the last suitcase the morning before we left. And thank heavens that I did because we learned that, at the time we had come over, duvets were not much known in Canada (rather, they had blankets and sheets), and so I was glad that I hadn't left our bedding behind.

On top of all the commotion, I developed a migraine headache and drugged myself to the point that I could hardly function. But I had to, and so I went on and finally got it all together, and were ready to part.

We celebrated Christmas Eve by ourselves, as we always had since we had Sabrina. We went to church, and after we gave Sabrina her little present. We had no Christmas tree but had our advent wreath with the four candles.

We said our goodbyes to Dietmar's parents on Christmas Day, and before we left, they promised that they would come to the airport for the final goodbye, and so we controlled our tears a bit in the hope to see them before our final departure.

When we visited my beloved foster-mother on the second Christmas holiday, the last few days before we left for Canada, it became heart-breaking since we knew we would probably never see her again. Everything was so final. I touched her face and felt her old, soft skin and saw her, for the first time in my life, really crying. Turning around so she couldn't see my tears, I asked myself "why," and somehow I hated myself for listening to Dietmar. I should have said no to it all.

With her, everything seemed so final because, at the time we immigrated to Canada, even a phone call was almost impossible. Oh, how I hated the situation.

My birth mother and her family joined us at my foster-mother's home, but to say goodbye to them was sad, but not painful. I was not close to her but after all she was my mother; however, I lived with her for only four years during my whole life. For me, my foster-mother was my angel; she raised me and gave me all her love until I was four years old when my birth mother took me away from her. But after the war ended, I returned, and I stayed with my foster-mother until I was twenty-one and got married. I loved my foster-mother as a child loves her birth mother and to part from her, knowing I may never see her again, was so very painful, and I could hardly think about it without breaking down.

Sabrina was confused; she knew that something was wrong, but she couldn't figure it out. My foster-mother gave her a new doll for Christmas, which somehow took us away a bit from our sorrow.

Unfortunately, when it was time to go, we realized the doll was too big to take on the plane, and so she couldn't take it with her. She cried bitterly, but it helped us to leave, because we were busy with her and somehow distracted.

A bit later, when we finally said our goodbyes, I held my foster-mother for the last time in my arms, and almost ran out of the apartment where I had lived most of my life and where my foster-mother gave me all the love she could give me.

I didn't know how we made it back to our apartment and how we lay later in our beds for the last few nights. I only remember that we couldn't sleep knowing we had to leave soon.

Leaving our homeland, the only land we knew and loved

On December 29, 1961 at the airport, we met most of Dietmar's family, my mother, her husband, and my half-brother, for the final time before we left for Canada. It was sad, but, in a way, we were all glad it was over because too many tears were shed already and made it so hard to say our final goodbyes without knowing when, if ever, we would see them again.

Our flight from Berlin-Tempelhof with Pan American Airlines to Brussels was called, and we went to the overhang towards the tarmac when suddenly a good friend of my in-laws came running towards us and wanted to give us oranges, a whole bag full of them. It seemed a goodbye present. He didn't hear the warning of the attendant, didn't stop running, and we didn't know how he made it. He was desperate to give Dietmar the big bag of oranges but was finally caught and told to return. However, he didn't and managed to reach us and, just like that, Dietmar had this big bag of oranges in his arms. Die didn't know what to do with it; we couldn't take it on board, and so he threw them over to a by-standing employee who almost caught the bag, but it fell and ripped, and all these beautiful oranges rolled all over. We saw how the man tried to collect them because oranges, at that time, were very expensive in Germany.

As we stepped onto the plane, we were so very embarrassed, but everybody who saw what happened had a big smile for us.

The flight to Brussels was uneventful, and I lost a bit of my fear of flying because, after all, it was my first time in an airplane. Sabrina, too, had no problems. We landed on time and had a five-hour stopover in Brussels where we were so happy to see Mrs. and Mr. Oka who met us and took us to their home for the time we had in between flights.

Kaeke and Lasse Oka were neighbours of my in-laws and had become very close friends, and so we, too, knew them very well. We celebrated many parties and had many dinners with them at my in-laws' house.

Lasse Oka was a Finnish diplomat and was transferred, a year before we left, to Brussels. They had two children, a girl named Eva, a bit older than Sabrina, and a two-year-old son named Kay; both were excited to meet Sabrina again.

We had a very pleasant visit, a nice break in-between flights, and the Oka's served a big dinner, and after, Dietmar could hardly move: he ate too much. Nevertheless, it was time to leave for the airport, and so we did.

In the car going back to the airport, Die complained and whispered that he was too full and didn't feel well. I was mad at him and told him to stop complaining. I answered, "And you ate too much." He whispered back, "I know, but I was hungry."

When we arrived at the airport, by the way almost too late, Dietmar looked as white as a wall. Lasse asked him if there was something wrong, but Dietmar answered, "No, no, I am only nervous." He held himself together and when he realized that we might have had too much luggage and would have to pay for the overweight, he held one of our handbags, which was as heavy as our suitcase, in his hand. (You wouldn't be able to do that nowadays, but at that time nobody took these things so seriously.)

We said very quickly our goodbyes (again) and were called to hurry.

We continued with Sabena Airline to the next destination, which took us to Montreal, then on to Toronto. It was the cheapest flight we could find and, of course, we took it.

Right after, we were finally in our seats, and the plane was in the air. Sabrina needed to go to the bathroom, and when I wanted to take her, the sign "Fasten your seat belts" came on. We had, right away, heavy turbulence and had to wait until the seatbelt signs were off. I was so afraid that Biena would pee her pants, but she was good and waited until we were able to make it this time.

Dietmar looked like he would die soon but didn't say too much.

Except for the turbulence at the beginning of the flight to Montreal, the flight was without any remarkable incidences until Dietmar who, by then, wasn't feeling good at all and needed badly to vomit but was too shy to use a bag. I didn't noticed his urgency, I was only concerned about my daughter when I guided her to the bathroom. Unfortunately, while sitting on the throne myself, we were caught in a terrible turbulence, and I became wet up to my waist. Sabrina screamed her head off and wanted to go back to her *Oma,* while I tried to clean and dry myself, and a flight attendant, who spoke a bit of German, knocked at the door and wanted to know if we were OK because she wanted us out to get to our seats as soon as possible.

I had to tell her what happened to me, but she insisted and said that we must come out. "Take the Kleenexes and try to dry yourself at least a bit. I will take your child to your husband and will come back to get you."

It was all easily said, but I had to wash and dry myself somehow and so when the attendant came back for me, I was in tears and very embarrassed.

Dietmar, by that time, had to vomit into a bag and looked utterly green in his face. He asked me what took us so long and while I tried to explain he rushed from his seat to the bathroom, and now I was waiting for him because the sign to fasten our seatbelts came on during another round of turbulence. Sabrina and I both became very scared, and I had my doubts that we would make it at all to Montreal.

Dietmar didn't return and, after a while, I was worried and practiced my English by asking a flight attendant if she could check on my husband. She returned quickly and told me that he was really sick but hoped that he would be returning soon. And sure enough, he came, looking awful, and it was so very embarrassing because he looked like he was tipsy.

I was angry with him since, first of all, he never drank and, secondly, I could not understand why he ate so much in the first place.

When he returned, Sabrina, of course, stroked his face, telling him that she is sorry for him, and said, "Papa, you will be better soon. Wait until we are home, I will help you."

Soon after, we calmed down, the turbulence stopped, and the flight became more or less pleasant.

Soon they wanted to serve dinner; we declined, and Sabrina fell asleep. Dietmar's face had colour again, and I went back to the bathroom to continue to clean myself. The flight attendants helped in bringing more tissues.

Returning back to my seat, Dietmar was himself again and apologetic to me because I was sure he was embarrassed too.

We all fell asleep, but after an hour or so, Sabrina woke me up by rattling on my arm, telling me that she was very cold. And she was right, I felt it, too, and I asked if I could have a blanket but was told that they had run out of them. The attendant gave us our coats.

An hour before landing, they served breakfast. Dietmar didn't eat. He told me that he felt better but didn't want to spoil it by eating. He wasn't hungry anyway, and Sabrina and I didn't eat much either.

Suddenly, everybody complained that it was bitterly cold in the cabin. The staff was very apologetic but said again that they were out of blankets.

Later, while departing, we learned that the opposite door of the cabin didn't properly close and in order to seal the door, they used all the blankets.

We passed the frozen blankets stuck together to an ice block, and holding the door closed and intact, and we heard that that was the reason why we were flying low so the door would hold up. It was a turbine prop machine, not a jet and, apparently, it could be done this way without any problems. I had no clue what they were talking about, but in learning all that, I was sure scared to continue our flight to Toronto before saying "We arrived safely."

The flight from Montreal to Toronto was OK, no problems whatsoever, and we landed delayed only by about twenty minutes. Not bad for an, all together, seventeen-hour flight.

Our arrival in Toronto

It was on Friday, December 30, 1961 when we arrived with our three-year-old daughter and three suitcases. Needless to say, from that moment on, our lives were about to change dramatically.

After we landed, we were asked to go to the immigration desk. We felt excited, strange sad, and like nobodies, and it was clear to us that we had to learn a lot to fit in.

The airport was at the time primitive (like a barrack) compared to the airport in Berlin-Tempelhof, which I think was the only building not damaged during the war and in full service, and it was the airport where later the Allies landed every three minutes to bring us food to survive the blockade.

I remember, we were the only people who landed as immigrants from that flight, and when we were at the counter we didn't know what to say or how to behave. Thank heaven Dietmar spoke a bit of English because the officer didn't speak German, but when Dietmar showed him our visa and the officer stamped it all over the place, he returned the papers with a smile and said, "Welcome to Canada" and showed us to the door. We were blank.

Thinking back, the whole immigration system was at that time so different and so much harder to settle in Canada. And yet, we made it as did many others too, since at one time or another, we all came from somewhere, and Canada became our new homeland. Let's face it, our family, like so many others, is now more Canadian than we ever were German.

But the beginning, until we called Canada our home, was a struggle.

Of course, times have drastically changed since. One can't compare it to 1961. We, for sure, were not welcomed by the Prime Minister or other dignitaries nor were we given warm jackets. (However, our circumstances were different; these people were refugees who came from Syria but still, the people who were welcomed didn't seem too needy at all.) (See an article from Douglas Todd: Trudeau goes silent on Syrian refugees.)

Relatives who wanted to follow had to go through the same paper trail as we had to, to get a visa. And if they were sixty-five years of age or over, old age pension was out of the question. There were no preferences, relatives or not. You were only eligible to get a pension if you worked here before. All immigrants had to do what Canadians did. They had no rights, and as I mentioned previously, the first priorities were to learn the language and integrate. Of course, we continued with our own customs which we were used to doing in our homeland, but not in public, only at home. We were still guests, and took the risk to make Canada our home, without help from the Canadian government.

It was hard! So many things were different to us.

The good thing was, Die had a job and that was our light at the end of the tunnel. He didn't know how much money he would bring home, another risk, but he told me that it would be all right. "Trust me," he always said. Well, I trusted him.

The company he was supposed to work for told him that he could support a family from his income, and if he showed that he could do the job as his papers showed he could, he would get a proper salary including health insurance, covering his family and himself. So, we knew that we would have no help at all, but since I believed my husband who was so sure that all would be good and that we were sure that we didn't need help, we gave it a try. I was hopeful, too, and tried not to regret our decision to come to Canada.

Again, the beginning was so hard and so very lonely. We were desperate to make it, and we tried very soon to blend in and prayed a lot, and looking back, our prayers were heard.

But nevertheless, we, too, were one of the lucky ones; we were also welcomed at Toronto airport but by a United Church German-speaking pastor, who greeted us by asking if we were the Steinkes, and after Dietmar confirmed, he continued, "I am glad that you finally made it and came out because I have been waiting here for you for almost over an hour." Later, he introduced himself as Pastor Horst. We looked at each other and smiled. I think he didn't realize that it had taken us almost seventeen hours to arrive in Toronto. What was one hour or so because, after all, we were so glad that we finally had land again under our feet.

We were too tired and didn't speak much, and again, our daughter wanted to go back home or to her grandmother. The pastor didn't notice at all that we were tired and babbled away while helping us with our luggage and guiding us to his car.

When we finally stepped out of the airport we saw some snow. Biena was so happy and excited about it that she pointed to the snow and said to her father, "Papa what is that?" Dietmar explained to her that it was snow and that we had it in Berlin, too, but since we had it warmer there, it snowed very seldom. She was fascinated with it, and we had somehow hoped that we would make it, and she would stop grieving about our family back home.

We were surprised to see that the pastor drove a Ford since, for us, this car was a dream. In Berlin, only American soldiers drove cars like that, and we thought he must be a very rich pastor. Or was he not the pastor? We were puzzled and surprised. Or did Dietmar translate "pastor" wrong; to us he didn't look like a pastor. So, Dietmar asked, "You are the pastor from the church, right?"

"Oh yes," he said, "I should have introduced myself properly! My name is Pastor Horst Weber and, yes, I am the pastor of the United Church in Toronto."

We took the Gardiner Express, which was, as Pastor Weber explained, brand new, and we realized that he was proud of it, and we were impressed. Berlin was very much in ruins, and so we thought maybe the airport was crummy but, in my mind, all was crummy. We forgave the airport situation.

He drove us to Boustead Avenue, close to High Park, and when he parked the car in front of a house he said, "We are here." I noted that the house didn't look bad from the outside, and was a little at ease.

Pastor Weber knocked on the door, an older couple opened it, and we were introduced to Mr. and Mrs. Robinson. They both looked friendly and asked in English if we had a good trip. We couldn't understand a word and looked for help from the pastor. With a smile, he translated and told the Robinsons that I didn't speak English but that my husband spoke a bit. He apologized for that because the Robinsons looked surprised. My husband at least said hello to them, and I stood there with Biena on my hand and was embarrassed. They talked again to the pastor, and he translated that they would like to show us the room, which was reserved for us by a man who had been asked to do so by the company that hired Dietmar. (Complicated, but thoughtful of the company.)

Telling Pastor Weber that the room was upstairs, Mr. Robinson stayed behind and apologized that he was not too well, and as Mrs. Robinson explained, he had a heart attack not long ago. Mrs. Robinson seemed very nice. She pointed to the staircase, and we all followed her and claimed the stairs up to the third floor, right under the roof, and opened a door, which was so low that my husband almost hit his head when he entered the room where we were supposed to live. It was very small, furnished with three beds, with little space in between and right beside in the corner with a small dresser. Of course, we learned later that it was a challenge to climb into and out of the beds without getting bruised. And a few nights later, we also learned that our love life was gone, too, because our daughter wanted to sleep in the middle bed. All so perfect, I had to fight back tears.

Behind the door was our "kitchen," a little table with a two-burner stove on top, and since there was no space left for our suitcases elsewhere, we placed them on the floor behind the door but after, we were hardly able to get in or out of the room.

I looked around and thought, *Welcome to Canada*, but said nothing to Die who I knew was upset as well.

There was some small talk between the pastor and Mrs. Robinson, and she wanted to leave, but before she left I asked, through the pastor, for the bathroom. She explained where I could find it and, again, the pastor translated to me that we had to go down to the second floor Mrs. Robinson wanted to leave. I think she was in a hurry because she could probably see our faces and the disappointment. My next question was where we could find her should we have further questions and, again, through the pastor, we were informed that most of the time she was in her kitchen, which was on the main floor. But after that, she hurried out and left.

A bit later, I looked for and found the bathroom, and learned that we had to share it with another tenant. When I returned and told Dietmar about it, we were both upset and looked at the pastor who wasn't upset nor surprised about our situation at all. Pastor Weber told us to calm and settle down first, and continued, "Get used to your surroundings and look for something more suitable later." He admitted this place was a "bit small" for the three of us but explained that when he was asked to find a place, it was for one person, not for a family with a very young child. McGregor phoned him about the change just three days before our arrival and he wasn't able to find something suitable in such a short time, he said smiling, but the company apologized for the inconvenience.

Before he left, he talked a bit about his church, where it was located and that there were some German members who would be pleased to meet us. My husband asked, "Members?"

"Yes, members. We here in Canada have a different system than, as I understand, you have in Germany. In Canada the churches are separate from the government and, therefore, are not supported by it. The churches here are paid for by the members of the congregation."

My husband looked at him. "How much is a membership?"

Pastor Weber answered with a straight face, "Usually ten percent of your income."

Dietmar smiled and answered, "I guess we will not go to church for quite a while. In Germany, as you know and mentioned, we pay taxes, including for churches, but I think we have to learn a lot in a hurry."

After that, the pastor suggested again to settle down a bit, but the most important thing is to learn to speak English. We thanked him for helping us that far, and he mentioned again, "Come and visit us at church, and if you need help, here is my card."

He left, and we were alone. We didn't say a word to each other until our daughter needed to go to the bathroom. Very urgent!

We all had to go to the washroom, and so I took Sabrina, and we stumbled down the stairs so Sabrina could go first.

I remembered where it was located and found it right away, but it was busy. We waited for a while, then I knocked. No answer. I knocked again and, finally, the door opened and an old lady came out. She said something to my daughter who started crying, and after Biena told me that she wanted to go home or to her grandmother and that she hated it here. Nevertheless, the old woman left, and we tried to go. Sabrina couldn't go and cried, "It hurts, Mami, I can't go here. I want to go home."

We realized that the old lady used the bathroom quite often and on top of that, she was hard of hearing, so that when we had knocked (or so we thought), she complained to my husband that we had been inconsiderate, which made me upset and angry. Dietmar talked to Sabrina, but without result, she only said, that she couldn't do her business quickly, and repeated, "I want to go home!"

Dietmar went to our landlady to complain. Somehow, she understood what he was talking about and gave him a potty. Our daughter who was toilet trained for the longest time had to use this potty again. It was so hard on her, and for us, too, but we had no other choice.

Taking a shower was another problem and almost impossible since, from the old lady's point of view, we took too much time. The best time for us to use the bathroom was maybe after lunch because she would have a nap or would go down to Mrs. Robinson's to have her tea. But since my daughter had a nap too, it always became a hassle and a problem.

Our first year in Canada

We realized how much we had to change and how different our customs were from the ones in Canada. What a culture shock! We were so alone, and every day became a new struggle, but we had to go on.

The next morning, on Saturday, we went to see Mrs. Robinson to ask her where we could go shopping. We were starving. She gave us some directions, it was hard because of the language, the shyness and insecurity one has when everything is strange. I was glad that Dietmar was able to speak a little and understood a bit of English and he was not shy to use it.

He took us to a coffee shop where we had some coffee and for Sabrina, chocolate, since she didn't like milk, and for each of us a sandwich with egg salad. The sandwiches were strange, too; they didn't serve dark rye bread. We knew we had to learn but wondered if we ever would. Die said that we would get used to it, and to not give up. We went to another store and bought potatoes and some other stuff, and later I cooked a meal. Like always, Sabrina didn't like it and wanted to go to her *Oma Meta*.

We all were very tired from the flight and, I guess, from the new surroundings, and so we got ready for going to bed early. We needed a bath or shower, but the bathroom door was locked and after waiting for half of hour or so, Dietmar went down to the Robinsons', and this time Mr. Robinson got in the action. Two minutes later, the old woman came out and said something to him; I think it was not pleasant, but he didn't seem to care, and I filled the bathtub for Biena.

We all were in bed by 7:00 P.M., and as I remember, we woke up by about 9:30 in the morning. And a new day began for us.

I made some breakfast and coffee, and for Sabrina, I prepared a fruit salad mixed with Kellogg's cereal. It was something completely new to her, but she liked it, and so it made my day.

It was New Year's Eve and very sad for us.

And again, Dietmar went down to Mrs. Robinson to ask her where downtown was, and she explained, I guess, very well because when he came up and told us that we could get to downtown Toronto, we were looking forward to going there.

I must say, he followed her directions without a blink. We went by streetcar from Roncesvalles to Dundas Street, and it didn't take too long to get to downtown. I think it took no longer than 35 minutes or so when Dietmar announced, "We are in downtown Toronto."

Getting off the streetcar, I looked around and asked, "I thought we were going to downtown Toronto?"

And Dietmar confirmed, making a funny face, which made us laugh, "I guess this is it."

We walked along on Yonge Street for a while, reaching Sears and Eaton's and noticed the windows were beautifully decorated like they were in Berlin around Christmastime, but what about all the other shops? Nothing, no decorations whatsoever and we noticed there were hardly any people around. We looked for a café (cafés were always open in Berlin) to get a cup of coffee and cake, but again, I think Toronto in 1961 had no cafés, except, maybe, a variety store, an ugly facility where we got only a cup of coffee and, for Sabrina, hot chocolate. Also, there were no tables, only a counter surrounded by some bar stools, and for us, it looked like a cold and awful place to be. The coffee we had tasted was like brown, lukewarm water and Biena's warm chocolate had not much taste either. No cake, they had only pie, and it looked so disgusting that Dietmar paid, and we left. I was sad, and Sabrina, like always, wanted to go home to Berlin, not as she said, back to where we had no bathroom.

We made it back all right and were hungry and tired, and I had prepared some sandwiches. For drinks, we had ginger ale, similar to a soft drink we knew from home. Biena had a good appetite and was tired, and when I put her to bed, she fell asleep at once.

Dietmar and I wanted to wait for the New Year to ring in, and so we sat on the bed and whispered to each other rather than talk. I

questioned Die what I should do on Tuesday, his first day at work and mine alone with our little daughter who wanted to go "home." He was a bit embarrassed and suggested that I should go out and get familiar with our surroundings and try to go shopping. We needed groceries.

"Try to talk to Mrs. Robinson. I am sure that she will help you."

"Talk? She wouldn't understand me, and I wouldn't understand her." We both laughed just thinking about it, but at least we laughed rather than cried.

Finally, it was a bit before midnight when Dietmar went to one of our suitcases and unpacked a bottle of wine. I was so surprised since I had no clue that we had wine in our luggage. He smiled with his cheeky little smile. "See, I am thinking about everything, and you doubt that we will make it in Canada."

We had no wine glasses, only cups, but better than drinking out of the bottle. He poured the wine and by the time it was twelve, I had no pain, but Die, who very seldom drank and was very sober, was glad that I wasn't crying. At midnight, we waited for the bells to ring in the New Year.

I should explain our custom in Germany, especially in Berlin, that at midnight all churches would ring in the New Year, and so we waited. But no bells here.

And so, tears ran down my cheeks again, and this time Dietmar's eyes were damp too.

We got over our sorrow and went to bed; we slept until Sabrina shook my arm to get up. She wanted breakfast, the same as she had the day before, and I was so happy that she had an appetite and was hungry.

Later in the afternoon, we went for a walk in High Park and when Mrs. Robinson saw us leaving, she wished us a Happy New Year. And as Dietmar told me, she asked how our first days had been and if we had found downtown. He thanked her and said that everything was fine.

High Park was very nice and was covered with snow which Sabrina enjoyed so much because again, in Berlin it snowed seldom, and for the first time she was laughing again and having fun. It made us happy to see her laughing because most important for us was to know that Biena could stop being so homesick. So when she laughed once in a while, we were glad; we hoped that she would forget her sorrow about being in Canada.

On Tuesday, Dietmar started his job, and Sabrina and I were alone and didn't know what to do. Mrs. Robinson came up and told me that if I need something I should come to her, and I spoke my first words in English and said, "thank you." It made me happy that I somehow understood what she told me and that she gave me a bit of encouragement to exercise my school English from a long time ago.

After our lunch and Sabrina's nap, we went for a walk, and later I prepared dinner. Not much, but we all had to eat, and Dietmar would be home by 5:30 P.M. and probably, after his first day of work in strange surroundings, he would be hungry.

When he stepped into the door, Sabrina jumped right into his arms, and we both were glad to see him. He had to tell us all about his first day at work, and I was happy to hear that he liked his new job a lot. Of course, there were many employees there who couldn't speak very good English either, but as he told me, had no problems and mingled in. I was glad for him but jealous since I had nobody, only my unhappy daughter and at times Mrs. Robinson, who tried so hard to make us smile.

A few days later I re-arranged our room a bit, so at least Dietmar and I could sleep together, and Sabrina had her bed on the opposite side wall.

I was glad that I had packed all our bedding because Biena told me that she liked her bed, it smelled like home.

I also went down to the Robinsons' and asked if we could get two chairs. She understood what I was talking about and helped to bring up both the chairs and a small table, and we could at least sit down to eat properly. One of us had to sit still on the bed and Dietmar volunteered, but Sabrina and I could sit down and had chairs. We could hardly turn, but it was so much more comfortable.

I learned that we were living in an area were many Polish immigrants settled down and when I talked to Sabrina while going for walks, we were looked down on. I realized that Germans were not welcomed here and that I had to be careful and was a bit scared.

Going shopping was another experience, it scared me do so because of my English. A problem, until I found a German delicatessen store where actually you could order in many languages not only in German.

Biena liked the store because at times, like my foster-mother did when she took Sabrina shopping, I bought a little something for her as well.

I was surprised at how cheap things were. When I bought some groceries here, I couldn't close my mouth at how little I had to pay compared to Germany, and I thought we might have enough to get by from whatsoever Dietmar's salary would be.

To buy vegetables was another story; I had to order in English because these stores, as I learned, belonged mostly to Polish people, and I was, as mentioned earlier, afraid of them. I would like to explain that during the war, my mother and I were evacuated by Hitler to Poland. Hitler believed that Poland would never be taken by the Russians, and so it was a sure haven to evacuate mothers and children to Poland while Germany was bombed to the ground.

After the war came to its end, and Germany was on its knees, the Polish people were liberated by Russia, and we were captured, sent to a jail and a bit later to a concentration camp, where we went through hell. The memories will never leave me and so, I was afraid to go into a Polish store where we, I was sure, would be treated like the Germans had treated them during the German occupation.

I wanted to buy cauliflower and found the word in my dictionary. I approached the store and, red-faced, practiced the word until I was in front of the sales clerk. Needless to say, I failed to say the word properly, and the sales clerk behind the counter realized my panic and asked in German how she could help me. I almost hugged her and told her my dilemma, but she laughed and pointed to the cauliflowers saying, "You should have taken one and brought it to the counter to pay for it."

I looked at her in disbelief since, in Germany, you never touched anything until a clerk would serve you and would hand the merchandise over to you after she had received your payment.

I remember that the lady in the vegetable store was very nice and taught me a bit about the Canadian shopping customs, which were so different from ours in Germany.

She also asked me where I came from, and how long we had been in Canada, and after telling her that we just arrived, she understood, and we talked about the war and how the Germans treated the Polish people, and we both realized what war can do to people and why there was still so much hate. She was an older woman, very pleasant, and we talked for quite a while. Her German was good and for me, it sounded like I was in heaven. She also mentioned that I could get everything we needed for groceries at Loblaw's, a big store not too far away from where we were.

"Go and try it," she said. "I shouldn't tell you that because the big stores take a lot of business away from us." She paused and smiled saying, "But you would have found out anyway. At Loblaw's, you don't need to talk," she explained. "You pick what you need and want from the shelves and after you have everything, you go to the cashier and pay for it. Try it, you will see, it is so easy."

"Thank you so much, it was great talking to you."

Smiling she answered in English, "You are welcome," and in German, "Come once in a while to say hi. It was nice to talk to you too."

When Dietmar came home that night, I told him what I had learned from the nice lady at the vegetable store about going to Loblaw's to shop. Again, he asked Mrs. Robinson for directions and since it was not far from us at all, we went on Saturday to try it out.

Wow, what a store! I couldn't close my mouth. The same with Dietmar, and we somehow realized we had no problems going shopping at all anymore. There, we had to grab what we needed, put it in a shopping cart and go to the cashier for payment. After we paid, the cashier would pack all the items into a big brown paper bag for us. What a thrill! Again, back in Berlin, we had to take our own shopping bags. So, what a difference, and when we went home, we were excited about our new experience. Sabrina noticed the self-serve as well and got excited about it too, yet she didn't understand that we had to pay for it. She thought she could take the things she liked without paying and so we had to watch her. I explained to her that if you take what you need from the shelves, they are not yours until you have paid for them. She looked at me and answered, "But at home, it is different, Mami. Here you can touch everything. At home, you always told me that I mustn't touch things before they are paid for."

"Yes, that's right. But here, you are allowed to touch and after you pay, they are so nice, and put everything you bought into a bag for you."

She was puzzled. She was confused, but she learned quickly. We had to stop her from taking things we didn't want, only the things we needed.

During the week, we were so lonely, and it was awful for us. Most of the time, we couldn't even go out; it was simply too cold. And so, we sat on our chairs, and I had to entertain my daughter somehow because she didn't understand what was going on and asked constantly why we couldn't go home.

"Don't you have to go to work?" she would often ask. "I want to go back to *Oma Meta*, I don't like it here, and they all speak funny."

Most of the time, we sat on our bed and watched the snow coming down or the squirrels hopping from one tree to the next. It was hard for Sabrina. She was an active child, and I was, at times, at the end of my rope. So, after the first week, I told Dietmar that Biena needed warmer clothes and some toys, crayons and drawing books.

"It might help her to forget her *Oma* and all the others, like your family."

Down he went to the Robinsons' and asked where he could buy things like clothes and toys for Sabrina, and Mrs. Robinson, never tired of helping, told him that we could go to Kresge, a store on Dundas Street.

Mrs. Robinson never gave up on us or our questions, and between my dictionary and her English to me, she understood, and I understood what we wanted from each other. It was funny at times, and we both laughed when we finally had it together, and I somehow lost my shyness in talking to her. She was always happy to help, and I never had the feeling I got on her nerves.

In Berlin, we had Woolworth after the war, which was loved by the Berliners. I believe it was a chain and well-known all over America but very new in West Germany.

On Saturday, we went to Kresge, and we were at home right away because it reminded us of Woolworth. We found what we wanted, and Sabrina got a snowsuit, boots and some toys, crayons and drawing books. And life became a bit easier for us during the week.

Dietmar got his first salary, which was $75, and as we realized, a very good salary. Oh yes, he made a lot more in Germany, but everything was so much more expensive there, and we knew very soon that if we spent the money wisely, we would be able to save $25 each week.

Almost every day, Biena and I went for walks, and I learned that Roncesvalles Street had a lot of European stores, in particular, a bookstore.

When we went into the store to look around. A salesperson came towards us to ask how she could help us, and I blushed and tried to explain that I wanted to look around first, but again, she answered in German that if I was in need of some help, she would be pleased to do so. Again, I was glad that we had found a store where we could speak German.

There they sold not only books, but a lot of things imported from Germany and later, for quite some time, the store became my favourite store. They even had a German book club called "Bertelsmann Book Club" that offered books through a catalogue, all in German.

At night, when Die came home, Sabrina and I were happy to see him and told him about all the new things we discovered.

I bought some books for Biena, and she asked right away if Dietmar could read a story to her before she went to sleep, and he assured her that he would.

He told us about his day at work and that he met the president of the company. Their meeting went well, and he felt good about it. The company expected a lot from him. But as he told us, "I will do fine. I have to manage the whole machinery department and about twenty-five people, mostly women. Many hardly speak English as well, only Italian or Portuguese and that, yes, is a challenge, but again, in time, I will do fine."

Almost two weeks had gone by, and I had to do a lot of laundry, and I had to speak to Mrs. Robinson to try to tell her that I had to do my laundry and ask where I could do it.

Back home I worked in the office for a laundry company and they looked after our laundry, and after a day or so and I had everything back, washed or cleaned.

We had no washers or dryers, so either we did our laundry by hand or we had it done. But I had no clue what to do here in Canada

and needed Mrs. Robinson to help, and I stuttered in my little English with the help of my dictionary what I needed to know.

"Oh," she said, after a while of finally understanding, "you can do that in our basement." She pointed to follow her, and we went down to the basement where she showed me the wringer washing machine and explained, "Here we are," thinking I would know how to operate the machine. I looked and wanted to say that I had absolutely no clue what I should do and tried to tell her, but she looked helpless too, and so we both gave up. I made her understand that I had to wait until my husband came home and maybe he could explain to me what to do.

A bit later, after Dietmar came home, and I had told him about my dilemma, the three of us went down to see her.

Mr. Robinson came as well, and so all of us went down to the basement. It was mostly dark by then, and I didn't feel too good without much light, even after she switched the lights on it was still dark. Sabrina didn't want to come. Dietmar took her by her hand and told her that there was nothing to be afraid of since we were all with her. Finally, she stopped complaining and came without letting go of Dietmar's hand.

Like myself, Dietmar, never saw a machine like that and told them so. They both looked at each other and smiling tried to tell us that this was a washing machine, pretty much safe to operate and in Canada almost every household has one, and Mrs. Robinson carried on saying, "Except if you want to give your laundry to a store to have it done, which is expensive." She continued to explain, "We don't wash laundry by hand except stockings etc."

Dietmar, after talking to me in German and to them in his broken English, asked Mrs. Robinson to explain how the thing works and after, tried to translate everything to me. But I still had no clue and became upset and turned to go upstairs. I thought that it was so hopeless, and I never would learn how to operate the stupid machine, but Die didn't give up. He called me back saying, "Bring your laundry down, and I will ask them to show us by washing it."

They agreed, and I left to take the pile down.

The Robinsons were so nice and patient in doing whatever they could to help us and even gave me some detergent to try it out.

We washed, with the help of the Robinsons, our first laundry in Canada, and I had no problems continuing with the second load by myself the next day. The only thing was, I was scared to hurt my fingers when using the wringer. But again, a week after, I was almost perfect at it. Being always dark in their basement, Biena was at first very scared but after she got used to it, she didn't mind coming with me any longer.

They didn't have a dryer, but the lines for hanging the laundry to dry were already in place, and Mrs. Robinson was so nice she allowed me to use her clothes pegs.

She told Dietmar that I could use the machine every day except on Fridays, which was her laundry day.

Sabrina, after watching me doing the wash a few times, started to like going to the basement, running around, playing with her ball and had fun watching me put everything through the wringer after the machine stopped washing our clothes. I had to make sure she didn't touch anything.

We both overcame our boredom by going for walks and going shopping, and I learned which stores were cheaper than others.

One day, Sabrina wanted a toy cash register like they had in the stores. "Will you play 'store' with me?" she asked.

I never saw a toy register anywhere and didn't know where to look for one since there were no toy stores in this area. But she didn't give up, she insisted on finding a store.

And so, out came my dictionary to find the correct word for cash register in English and afterwards to remember it. Sabrina remembered the word faster than I did by listening to my practicing but I think that was not too important because first of all I had to find a store and then ask a sales clerk if they carried something like that, which for me was always the most embarrassing part of going shopping.

We walked along Roncesvalles Avenue, and Sabrina pointed to the variety store and said, "Mami, they have toys. Maybe they carry a toy cash register." So in we went, and after trying out my few words of English, the young sales clerk smiled and handed me a toy register. Biena was beside herself and said, "See Mami, I told you we would find one." And I was happy, too, and after I paid for it, we both walked out of the store as if we were carrying a trophy.

For a few days, we were very busy and played "store," and didn't walk much, but as it goes with all toys, it became boring after a while, and a short time later, we started with our walks again.

One day, we visited the bookstore I liked so much and found a dictionary, called *1000 Worte in Englisch* (1000 Words in English), a special German-English dictionary, which also showed how to pronounce English words. So, of course, I bought it at once.

Well, what a wonderful tool to learn the language with. I couldn't believe my luck after I tried it out on Mrs. Robinson.

First thing, when Die came home, I told him about my purchase. I was so excited that I jumped up and down and hugged him and kissed him, and I think, for a change, I was happy. And so was Biena because she, too, told her father that we had had a good day, which she had never told him before.

Now, every day after lunch, when Biena had her nap, I practised learning English, and with the help of the new dictionary I read an easy to read English novel. Since this little book was a love story and very simple, I understood after a while a lot more than I thought I would have, and also I was not too afraid to talk if I had to. Mrs. Robinson was the person I mostly tried out my bit of English on without being embarrassed. She was so nice, and I had the feeling that she understood me when I asked for something without rushing. I always admired the patience she had with me. Often, she helped by repeating the word or sentence so that I would learn better by hearing a word again. I started to love her.

The winter was hard and often we were not able to go out. We had a lot of snow, and it was too cold, and not being used to temperatures like that, we stayed in. Mrs. Robinson must have noticed and asked us down for a coffee or tea. I didn't want to be impolite, and so we went. The old lady, who made our life complicated because she used the bathroom too often was there, too, and the TV was running. Most of the time we didn't understand a word until something funny happened and understanding or not, we had to laugh.

Mrs. Robinson was happy for us when she heard us laughing because she even mentioned to Dietmar that we were always so sad-looking, and she was worried about us. So, I think when she realized we had a bit of fun we made her happy.

We didn't stay long because I didn't want to overstay our time with her. But when we said our goodbyes, and I thanked her for the invitation, I think she said, "Come again. TV is good for the two of you!"

We went back to our room, Biena seemed happy and said, "Mami, this was funny when this one man hit the other two with a frying pan over their head. Can we go tomorrow for coffee again? I have to tell Papa about it."

And sure enough, Dietmar stepped into the door, and she ran right into his arms.

"We had such a nice day. We saw three funny men hitting each other with a frying pan, and you should have seen their faces, it was so funny. Right, Mami?"

I had to explain her excitement and about our little visit with Mrs. Robinson and that I thought she had invited us again. I guess that was what she had meant.

"She is a very nice person, I like her. By the way, the old lady was also there, but she always looks at me as if I come from the moon."

We all laughed and had our dinner. Never much because, what can you cook when you have only two pots and no space to put things? But it was better than before when we didn't even have plates or cutlery, and Die had to go and ask for them. Mrs. Robinson gave him three of each, like glasses and plates etc., apologizing that she hadn't thought about those things at all.

We had at least enough dishes so we could eat together.

My birthday was on January 15, and I was not in a good mood because Dietmar didn't even wish me a happy birthday before he left. He must have forgotten what day of the month it was, and I was down, homesick. It was hard for me not to show my mood to Sabrina because she, too, wanted to go home and missed her *Oma Meta*.

We went out for a while but had to come home soon because of the weather, it was awful and very, very cold.

On our way up to our room, Mrs. Robinson called us in for a cup of coffee and for Biena, hot chocolate. Of course, we accepted at once. We watched a bit of TV, and I started to cry; my tears came out without me being able to stop them. Mrs. Robinson took me in her arms and probably said nice words, but I just couldn't stop. I think I

felt sorry for myself, and she let go of me. She went to her living room and returned with a glass of whisky, and said, "Here, drink, that will help." And after the third glass, I had no pain at all. We laughed, and I didn't know over what, but I noticed she was drinking, too, and so we both were happy, including Sabrina who had some fruit juice.

It was getting dark outside, and I wanted to return to our apartment when Dietmar came home with a little bouquet of flowers in his hand and wished me a happy birthday. Mrs. Robinson was surprised and told Die the mood I was in but then jokingly said, "A husband should never forget a birthday or anniversary!" He translated all that to me, and I went over to her and gave her a hug.

Dietmar asked her for a nice place to get some dinner.

"I am sure Steffie hasn't cooked, and so I have to take my two ladies out to get something to eat." He took us both in his arms, and we left. It snowed badly, but I was not too sober and Sabrina laughed when her father threw a few snowballs at her. We made it to a little restaurant, and we had a small meal.

My first birthday in Canada was not bad after all.

We had been in Canada for one month, and we both needed a haircut. Like always, Dietmar went to Mr. Robinson to ask for a barber, and I went to Mrs. Robinson to ask for a hairdresser. Dietmar had luck because Mr. Robinson went to one not too far away and when Die tried the barber out, he came back not too bad looking.

To find the right hairdresser for me was another story because Mrs. Robinson wore her hair in a bun and didn't need a hairdresser. She cut and washed her hair herself like my foster-mother did in Germany.

The next day, Biena and I went for our walk and found a hairdresser on Bloor Street, not too far away either. The question was, how will I tell her or him what I wanted and when could they take me? In Germany, we never made appointments for either a doctor or a hairdresser; we went and waited for our turn. But Dietmar overheard the girls at work talking about appointments.

The girl in the hair salon spoke a bit of German, and I made an appointment for the next day, which I will never forget.

I explained to her how I wanted my hair cut, but she must have suddenly forgotten her German because after she cut my hair, and I looked in the mirror, I couldn't believe my eyes. She cut it much too short and when we returned home, I combed my hair over again and again, almost until Dietmar had come home. There was no dinner on the table, no nothing, only a bad, bad mood. Die, like often, laughed and told me that I didn't look too bad at all and that he loved me, and it will grow again. And, of course, Biena said, "Papa, I told her that too. But I don't like it, and I am hungry!"

We both had to laugh.

When we went down and met Mrs. Robinson, she looked at me strangely. I knew it was my hair, and I swore I would never go to that hairdresser again. And I didn't. Later, I learned to do my hair myself; I even cut my hair, and it looked good. I saved a lot of money.

I wrote letters to either my *Muttchen* or to my mother-in-law almost every second day, and so we got back a lot of mail from Germany as well. They both were worried about us, and especially my *Muttchen*, who missed having Sabrina during the day.

Both always mentioned the situation in Berlin. They confirmed the stories we read in the German newspaper, a paper we discovered in the German delicatessen store.

It didn't change. Many people still fled, at risk of being caught. The strict regime in the East stayed strong. It was like a dictatorship all over and if you were not politically correct, you were put into jail. Awful!

My mother-in-law wrote that we should be glad that we were in Canada.

Were we? Many times, I thought it was a big mistake to have left everything behind to come to Canada. But Die never complained, he seemed happy and content. My problem was to entertain Biena during the whole day and very much so to learn the language.

Mind you, I had picked up many words but I was still embarrassed to speak because I knew my pronunciation was way off.

Mrs. Robinson invited us every often to come down to watch so many shows on TV, shows like *The Three Stooges* and *The Andy Griffith Show*, which were very easy to understand. By watching the movements of the actors, which was at times funny by itself, and the easy language used, it explained what was going on. Biena had a ball because I think she understood more than I did.

We still walked a lot and at the beginning, winter didn't seem to end, but after February, it warmed up, and later, we had a bit of a

routine that included Biena's nap and my reading and learning English at the same time.

One day in early March, Mrs. Robinson explained to me that the apartment below, with a full kitchen and a bedroom or living room, would become available and asked if we would be interested in having it. I asked her how much more it would be, and she answered that the difference would be $10 per week more than what we were paying. I told her that I would have to talk to Dietmar first but would let her know a bit later.

Right away, I figured that we could afford the increase. With Dietmar's salary, we would have $50 extra, so we could afford it. But before I talked to Die, I went back to Mrs. Robinson to ask her how much it would be if we kept the room upstairs as well because, that way, we would have a kitchen and a little living room plus the bedroom upstairs. She looked at me, and I wasn't sure if she had understood what I meant, but then she answered, and as I understood it, it would still be $25 per week. And she continued that we could also use the second bathroom on that floor, rather than sharing one with the old woman.

"Oh!" I jumped, and told her again, "We will let you know tonight."

I was hardly able to wait for Die to come home that night. I was beside myself thinking about having more living space and a kitchen and the most important, our own bathroom.

So when Die came home, he saw right away that something good happened.

But, before I could even say something, Biena yelled right away, "Papa, Papa, we are moving, we will have a kitchen!"

He looked at me, and I finally had a chance to tell him the news myself. He was happy, too, but somehow worried that we were not able to afford the change and asked right away, "How much do we have to pay for the apartment?"

"It will be altogether $25, which includes the upstairs bedroom and our own bathroom. We will have to see the Robinsons."

She needed to know by that night, and I thought I understood everything correctly.

After dinner, the three of us marched down to hear the news once more, and have a look at the apartment to decide if we wanted to move.

They had had their dinner, and we were asked to sit down for a moment until the table was cleared. Mr. Robinson helped her but said, "I had better leave you because my wife is responsible for renting out the rooms. I only do maintenance," and with a smile, he left us, and we learned who the boss was regarding business in that household.

Dietmar led the conversation, but I told him earlier what to ask, which was to see the apartment and if we liked it, whether we had to sign a lease.

She took us to the first floor and showed us the apartment and explained to Dietmar that, no, we didn't have to sign a lease since we had to take it as it was without any renovations etc.

Compared to what we had and what we would have had if we had moved down to the second floor, it was like heaven. The kitchen was large and had two windows with a view of the backyard, and the living room was not too bad either. After a few minutes of thinking things over and making sure that I understood everything correctly from when I had talked to her in the morning, that a bathroom with the tub and the upstairs bedroom would be included in the price of $25 per week, we agreed to take it.

Since the kitchen was equipped with pots and utensils, and a table and four chairs, we didn't have to buy anything at the moment and could move in the following Monday.

And after Dietmar painted the kitchen on the weekend, and it looked fresh and clean, we were happy with our decision.

On Monday, I went down and cleaned and scrubbed the kitchen cupboards and the living room, and with the help of my daughter, we were proud to serve our first dinner that night, sitting properly down and enjoying every bite. Even Biena didn't complain that I didn't cook like her *Oma*. Our upstairs bedroom got a clean-up as well, and the kitchen stuff, the chairs and the table went down to the Robinsons' basement again.

We changed our bedroom by dividing it with a curtain around Biena's bed, which she liked very much because she felt that she had her own little room, and we felt we had a bit of privacy as well.

My worries, in general, became a bit less until I realized my period hadn't come, and my first thought was that I was pregnant.

What a thought! It was awful to think about being pregnant and then dealing with it in our situation. I didn't tell Dietmar about it, but when I counted the weeks and was more than six weeks overdue, I became scared and couldn't hide my emotion any longer. I thought, *what should I do?*

I finally told Die and cried my heart out, but looking up, I saw that Die was not upset a bit and said, "We will cope with it. Maybe your period will come a bit later; it is not that much over the time."

"I hope you are right, but I am never late."

"Oh, Steffie, you worry about everything!" And he took me in his arms and I felt better.

The next day, I looked up in my dictionary and practiced my English with words like diapers, crib, etc. and I felt so sorry for myself that even Sabrina became worried, but I had to tell her that I was fine.

Mrs. Robinson was always kind and wanted to help wherever she could. Compared to Mr. Robinson who was happy if you didn't bother him since, I think, Sabrina was a bit much for him. He tolerated her and, surprisingly, she liked him a lot. She spoke in German, and he answered in English, and I felt they both understood what they were talking about. But, I had a feeling he was not too keen on listening to her babbling.

The Robinsons had no children of their own and practically had to learn how to cope with a child at Sabrina's age, which was not easy in general, so for them, I was sure it was a huge adjustment.

On the weekend after our move, Dietmar asked Mrs. Robinson where we could find a furniture store. We wanted to buy a sofa, two chairs and a coffee table for the living room.

Again, she was happy to help.

"Go to Kresge first, and if you don't like what they have, go to a furniture store not too far away from Kresge, also on Dundas Street."

We entered the Kresge department store first, and I went straight to the baby department, but in the end we found a chesterfield set and a table in the furniture store, not too much to our taste since the European taste differed a lot from the Canadian, but it was not bad, and actually more a Scandinavian style. Mrs. Robinson really liked it and after we got used to it, we liked it too.

But still, we were surprised about how reasonably everything was priced. Mind you, not so much for us, since we lost a lot of money when we had to exchange our DM into Canadian dollars. But yes, we were amazed at what we got for a dollar when we went grocery shopping and that was from the money Dietmar earned in Canada.

Two weeks later, I had my period, and I was absolutely beside myself. When Die came home that night, and I told him, he, too, was happy, and since Dietmar couldn't tolerate alcohol, we celebrated with a bottle of Coke.

Life was not too bad, but we often were very homesick, and I was so very lonesome, and I sometimes shed my tears when Sabrina had her nap.

I think it was at the beginning of March when I had a toothache. Right away, I realized that it was one of my wisdom teeth, and I needed to see a dentist, and Mrs. Robinson helped by making an appointment for me. It was not too far from where we lived, and she offered to watch Sabrina while I was gone.

A new experience and a new challenge.

For instance, back home there would be almost no snow in March and nobody would ever take off their shoes going to a public place or office. And so, without giving it a thought, I marched into the office and tried to explain that I had an appointment and needed to see the doctor.

Apparently, Mrs. Robinson told them that I could hardly speak English, and the nurse answered in German that I had to wait for a moment but asked me to take my boots off. I looked at her thinking I was in the wrong place. I took them off anyway, and she came and cleaned up the big puddle. After, I understood what she was talking about and was very embarrassed, and when I looked around, I saw the faces of the other patients who, by the way, sat there without boots, with only their socks on.

The dentist had a look, poked around, which hurt so much that I almost screamed, and tried to tell me that my tooth should come out, but he couldn't do it since I already had a bad infection. He gave me antibiotics and told me that I should see him again in three days. The next day my face was so swollen that I went back to him without an appointment. He looked again and advised that I had to see a specialist at once. His assistant took me out and made the arrangement to see a surgeon, who had his practice on University Avenue. She explained that I needed some surgery done right away, and all I could say was that she should call Mrs. Robinson since I didn't have any idea what was going on and where I should go. The nurse was nice and realized that I had no clue and called Mrs. Robinson to give her the details and that I needed help soon. She told me to go home and assured me that Mrs. Robinson would take care of me.

Shortly after I arrived back home, Mrs. Robinson was already waiting for me. She had one look at me and knew at once that there wasn't much time, saying, "We have to go, the appointment is in one hour, and we have to take the streetcar to University Avenue." I was almost in tears because I hardly understood what she was talking about, but Mrs. Robinson had no patience and practically pushed me out the door. I heard Sabrina asking for me, and yet again she pointed to Mr. Robinson. I mentioned Dietmar, but she answered, "there is no time."

We made it to the streetcar and were soon on our way. My pains were almost unbearable, and I couldn't see out of my left eye anymore. Mrs. Robinson went to the front and talked to the conductor who turned around and moved his head as if he said "yes" to her. I didn't really know how we arrived but noticed that the streetcar stopped somewhere, but not at a stop. We got off and walked across the street and entered a building.

I was taken in at once, and they gave me a needle and my pains were gone and later, all I felt was a big package in my left cheek, realizing that my wisdom tooth was gone. I figured that I had an anaesthesia and was asleep while the surgeon removed the tooth but wasn't sure.

When I looked up, Mrs. Robinson was sitting beside me, and a doctor talked to her, and all I understood was the words "pain later." She looked after me as if I was her daughter. She helped me to get into my boots and my coat and left the office to go to the streetcar stop, this time on our side. We had to wait a bit, but not long. Somehow, I didn't feel too bad at all when we entered the streetcar but a while later, I guess the anaesthesia wore off. I was in so much pain that Mrs. Robinson ran to the conductor, and a bit later he stopped the streetcar where she got off and ran across the street to a drugstore. People stared at me, but I was helpless, and the pains were almost too much bear so much that tears were running down my cheeks but regardless, I guess everybody was upset because of the interruption. After about ten minutes, I saw her running out of the store, almost causing an accident, holding a bag in one hand and in the other a little container of, I assumed, water. She hopped on, and we were moving again. She gave me two tablets and talked to me. A few minutes later my pains were bearable.

I didn't know where we were or how she managed to make the conductor stop the streetcar, but she did. (This wouldn't happen now, but I guess it was different in 1962.)

Arriving at home, she helped me up and undressed me, and I fell asleep at once.

Later, when Dietmar came home, she caught him at the door and told him the whole story. He was so thankful to her but was as puzzled as I was. When he later asked me why I didn't phone him, I told him I didn't know the phone number.

"Oh yes, I forgot to give you and the Robinsons my telephone number from my work, and not only that, I have forgotten the number as well. I will correct it at once tomorrow. I realize now how important it is that I can be reached in an emergency. And I will ask the Robinsons for theirs as well because I saw they have a telephone."

The next morning before Dietmar went to work, Mrs. Robinson came up and asked him how I was and told him that, if it was OK with us, she would look after Sabrina.

"Don't worry," she said. "Everything will be fine. Call me during the day. I will let you know how we are doing."

Dietmar was so relieved that she helped us because he didn't know how he could manage the situation with his new job etc. and told her again how thankful we were.

I was much better after two days, and with the tablets, it healed fast.

We received the invoices for all the expenses a few days later, and were so glad that we took the insurance, which was recommended by the person at the Canadian embassy in Berlin.

Our new life in Canada

Spring arrived slowly in April, and somehow our life in Canada became livable.

Sabrina and I eventually became familiar with our surroundings, and when we went for walks, we were sure we would find our way back home again.

I learned how to speak a bit more English every day and wasn't too scared of speaking, regardless how it came out, correct or wrong.

Mrs. Robinson was so very supportive and would often correct me, which I didn't mind at all. When I spoke, and she was able to understand what I was talking about, I was glad that she did.

Sometimes Sabrina went down to their place, and I found her in the kitchen talking to the Robinsons or watching TV. She didn't ask me, she just sneaked down, and I was upset since I wasn't sure if she was a nuisance; however, Mrs. Robinson always assured me that she was welcome at any time. "She is so funny and makes us laugh and, I must say, she is very well behaved. I will let you know when we go out or something, don't worry."

It was at the beginning of May when Die bought a tricycle for her. He came home with it as a surprise. (For the both of us.) At first, I was not amused because I thought I was the one who had to watch and run after her when Dietmar was at work, but she learned quickly and, yes, became fast with it. She was happy to go out, and even mingled and played with the kids on the street.

She laughed again and that, for us, was like a blessing to see our daughter happy without always asking when we were going back home and when she could see her *Oma Meta*.

In 1962, kids could play on the streets without constant super-vision by grown-ups, and so for short times I could go upstairs and watch her from the kitchen window. What a change for me and her. Her English improved by the day, and soon she answered in English, and I couldn't understand what my daughter said, but I learned as well.

It was about mid-May when we received a letter from Dietmar's mother that she would be coming to visit since she missed us and hoped it would be all right with us.

Well, what a surprise! And where would she sleep, and how would she like it here, and how would we entertain her? And a thousand ques-tions more. We were both in panic, but very excited to see her. Since she had already booked the flight we had two or maybe even three weeks to make plans.

She wrote that all she needed was a letter from us confirming that we agreed to keep her for the duration of three weeks as a visitor to get the visa for Canada. We went down to the Robinsons' and tried to explain the situation and if they might have a room for her and that we need it only for two or three weeks, the length of her visit. They had one room, and we reserved it for $20 for two weeks. We realized it was expensive, but maybe better than a hotel room. We were happy that mother had her own room in the same house. Mother stayed three weeks, and Mrs. Robinson charged only the $20 she originally wanted to have for two weeks. How nice of her.

When we told Sabrina about the visit, she jumped up and down and yelled, "My *Oma* Else is coming, my *Oma* Else is coming!"

It was sure exciting, and we all couldn't wait to have her.

We picked Mother up from Toronto airport at the beginning of June, and we all were so very happy to see each other again. Sabrina was beside herself; she wouldn't let go of her hands, and at night, she would sneak to her bedroom and the two of them would snuggle up, falling fast asleep.

Die couldn't take time off, and so it was my job to entertain his mother. I was afraid that it would be hard, but it wasn't at all. We had a jolly good time together and became closer than we ever had been before.

She liked it very much in Canada and was very appreciative for every day she had with us.

She loved High Park and the park was absolutely gorgeous in June, and so we went there at least every second day for long walks.

She also mentioned that she noticed the houses and neighbourhood around us were so unique and different from the houses in Berlin.

We went to Lake Shore to the big swimming pool and Sabrina and her *Oma* Else didn't mind that it was a bit cool; they had their fun, regardless if it was cool or not.

Coming home from an outing, my mother-in-law needed her ever-so-strong coffee right away, and after, she helped me with cooking the dinner.

When Die came home, she and Sabrina couldn't tell him quickly enough what we did and how our day was, and my husband was glad that his mother liked everything in Toronto.

Dietmar thanked me, as he said, for doing a great job of entertaining his mother and gave me a wonderful bouquet of flowers. Yes, that was my Die; he always appreciated our love for each other and our life together. Never took anything for granted.

I took his mother to the museum, and Biena was bored but was gracious enough to ask only me if we could get out of there because she didn't like most of what she saw and told me it was boring.

On weekends, Die took over, and we went downtown to see Eaton's and Sears and Else too mentioned that, compared to Germany, everything was so much cheaper. She thought she was in paradise because Berlin was still showing a lot of the lost war, so yes, everything was very, very expensive and was often out of reach for ordinary people to have. She liked our streetcars and how polite people were. She liked walking on Yonge Street; she was fascinated with almost everything there was, so it was not hard at all to please her, which was my biggest fear before she came to visit.

We talked often about the East and West situation in Germany, and she told us that so many people tried to escape from the east side of Berlin. They built tunnels, and for a while quite a lot of people were able to escape without being harmed. But after the East found out about the tunnels, the shooting started again, and the borders became tighter than ever, and it was impossible not to be caught. My mother-in-law said, "It is almost like we had it in Hitler's time. East Germany is like a camp, surrounded by a wall and even guarded by dogs, mostly

German shepherds." She always ended her talk about the situation in Berlin by saying, "Be glad you are here. Oh, I believe you miss us, so do we, but you live in peace here, and you will make it. The next time I come, you will have moved to a nice apartment." We smiled and said, "We will try! But at the moment, the worst thing is not to be able to speak much English."

She loved going grocery shopping. For her, Canada was a dream country, and she found the Canadian people relaxed and so very friendly. And she was right, they were, not only the Robinsons but most of them.

Canadians were so anxious to help as soon as they realized that you were an immigrant and couldn't speak English yet. We always felt welcome here and very seldom not so welcome. As I mentioned before, around us lived many Polish immigrants, and I understood that they were not too friendly but angry because they or their relatives suffered so much during the war. So, often they looked down on us if they realized that we came from Germany, and when I heard at times that Biena had a fight with them, I told her to come home at once. She always did, except one time when she was clobbered badly. Mrs. Robinson went to their parents and after that, the kids were fine. I didn't know what was said, but I guessed the children had been told by their parents to stop hitting Biena, and after a short time they even played together.

Die's mother became sad that the time to fly back home arrived faster than we realized. The three weeks were over in no time, and she packed her suitcase. We were all so very sad, but she promised to be back soon and so with much sadness and hope to see her again, we took her to the airport, which she didn't criticize like we had when we first arrived in Toronto. She said, "The next time, Toronto will probably have a new airport because I saw that they were working on it."

There was an emptiness in our apartment after she left, and we felt lonely again. Sabrina and I felt like we were in a place we sure didn't belong.

Biena would ask, "Mami, why did she leave and didn't take us with her?"

I thought the same thing. I answered, "Because we are living here and all our other loved ones stayed in Berlin. *Oma* Else had to go back because she has to cook for them."

What else could I have said to her?

She looked up at me with her big, brown eyes and asked, "Why?"

It was hard to make her understand, but I knew that we both were very homesick.

I didn't tell Die about our feelings because I knew it would make him feel guilty and maybe homesick too.

I assumed he liked everything in Canada, including his job and, if not, he would never complain; after all, it was his idea. Yes, I had agreed to it as well and so we had to take it like it was.

One day I saw Dietmar in the backyard talking to Mr. Robinson. Sabrina was with him, but it seemed to me that he wasn't paying much attention to her because she must have asked him something, and she took his hand, wanting to go somewhere, yet he carried on talking. After a while, they all walked slowly to the shed where they disappeared for quite some time.

I was busy with cooking and forgot about it.

Later, when Die and Biena came into the kitchen, Sabrina ran straight to me, telling me excitedly that we had bought a car. I thought for a moment that I wasn't understanding right because sometimes when she got excited, she talked in her baby language. So, I looked at Dietmar and said, "Did I understand correctly? Did you buy a car?"

"No," he answered. "Not yet. You know that I wouldn't buy anything like that without talking about it first with you," and smiling at me, he continued, "I mean with my 'finance minister.'"

That was my Die. If he wanted something, he knew how he could play me. Regardless of what it was, I hardly could say "no." But this time I was on the defence, and so was he. He was prepared for it and said right away, "Steffie, I know what you want to say, but I think we should buy it. It is a 1956 Ford and since Mr. Robinson had his heart attack, the car has been stored in the shed on blocks. It has only 2400 miles on it, and is practically brand new."

"How much?"

"That's the thing, only $350."

"And what would it have cost new?"

"I don't know, but I will find out. I think they are between $1500 and $1600. You have to see it. It would be good for us; we would be able to make trips. I would, as always, use the streetcar to go to work, but on weekends, we could learn what our surroundings look like. People at work tell me that Ontario has a wonderful landscape."

"First of all, Dietmar, if we spent $350 from our savings, we would have $150 left, and who knows if that would be enough should we need money for an emergency. Secondly, as you know better than I, a car costs money to run, gas and upkeep, etc. At the moment, we have enough money, but what if we want to move into an apartment, I mean in an apartment building, where we have real privacy, not like here where we still live in someone else's house. Thirdly, you have no driver's licence. Think about it, and think hard because, like always, you see only the good; you don't think about what might come later."

He laughed and answered, "That's why I married you," but quickly continued, "That was a joke. You know I love you! I will have to get my driver's licence, but I am sure that that will be no problem. Please have a look at the car. And by the way, I assure you, money-wise, we will make it just fine. My boss has already talked about a raise within a month or so."

The next day, Dietmar asked Mr. Robinson if he could show the car again. "Steffie wants to see it too."

To make it short, we bought the car, and I think it was the best thing we ever did.

The car was in a very good condition and so big that our little Fiat back in Berlin would have fit into it without problems.

Sabrina said, after the deal was completed, and we sat down in our kitchen, "See Mami, I told you that we bought a car!"

Her father smiled without saying anything.

These two always had it in for me, and I loved them so much for it.

Our New Car

Dietmar received his driver's licence within a week and without any difficulties. He told me it was so much easier than in Germany. He had absolutely no problems.

The rest of the summer was great. We made a lot of tours and enjoyed every trip.

Mrs. Robinson mentioned their cottage and offered to rent it to us for the weekend for $10.

Dietmar was familiar with cottages. He said to me that before we had met, he had been in Finland on vacation for three months where the people he lived with had a cottage.

I think that was why he was so crazy about Canada, because of the similarity to Finland's landscape. He was so excited and looking forward to going to a cottage that I gave in and started packing for the weekend. I remember it was close to Peterborough, and he was sure to find it easily, which, to my surprise, he did.

It was dark when we arrived, and we tried to find the bedroom since Biena had fallen asleep in the car.

The cottage was freezing cold, and the sheets on the double bed were only sheets without even a blanket. I was glad that I had brought the bedding for Sabrina with me, so she at least could be warm in her bed, which was a little couch.

When we settled down, Dietmar and I were constantly fighting for the sheets, and we hardly slept.

During the night, Sabrina had to go to the washroom. It was then we learned that there was none. Instead, we had to use the outhouse, and Sabrina and I refused to go there because, not being familiar with the property at all, we hardly knew what we might step in. In the end, we all peed outside and marched right back into the cottage, where, after, Dietmar had finally found his flashlight.

An hour or so later, Sabrina suddenly stood in front of us and said, "There is a noise close by, and it scares me." We listened and heard it, too, when Dietmar said, "Oh, I think those are coyotes or wolves. After all, we are in Canada, in the wilderness here."

"What did you say, wolves?"

"Well, it could be."

He was very cool and collected about it, and I was scared and very worried and asked, "What if they attack us?" We all stayed awake until the sun came up.

Later, we learned that the howling wasn't from wolves or coyotes but from loons.

In the morning, after maybe three hours of sleep, we opened the door and saw for the first time the beautiful landscape, the wilderness, and the lake.

We were so happy to be there. Gone were the strange noises and worries that we might be attacked by wolves or coyotes. We were simply amazed. Sabrina loved it too.

Going fishing with her father for the first time, learning how to, and after a while, catching a fish was an absolute wonder for her, and she was the happiest child under the sun.

But I went back to the cottage and started cleaning. Not knowing that cottage life was different from city life; in other words, you should enjoy the outdoors and should only be inside if the weather is bad, but I thought the cottage was dirty and needed cleaning. Of course, it was not, it was a rustic, beautiful little cottage without a bathroom but with water inside coming from the lake. That was why Mrs. Robinson told Dietmar to bring fresh water from home. She even gave him a container, which I questioned, but Dietmar explained that we shouldn't drink the water from the tap.

We had a wonderful weekend, and later, when we rented the cottage again, we made it our home for the short time we were there, by bringing our own stuff for the weekend or later, even for a week of holidays.

To this day, our first time in cottage country is a memory I never will forget. So wonderful; strange, but wonderful!

Dietmar and Sabrina were in their elements, and I learned quickly to enjoy and love that different life as well.

A few weeks later, I discovered that, next door, new people had moved in, and right away I thought they looked like and spoke German.

I told Dietmar about it, and he was excited to hear the news, and not much later that week, after Die came home, he went to meet them and, sure enough, they had come from Stuttgart, Germany. They arrived in Canada two weeks earlier and seemed very friendly. He invited them up for coffee, and we hit it off right away.

Neither spoke a word of English, which made me feel better because I could talk to them and was understood. They hadn't been married long, had no children, and only had to look out for themselves. I think that made it easier to start in Canada.

Since they had no car yet, we arranged for sometimes, and when they wanted to, that they would join us on trips but would share the cost of the gas. It became a pleasant and nice arrangement.

Their names were Gunter and Ushi, and they became our first close friends here in Canada.

Gunter was a carpenter/cabinet maker and found work very easily, however Ushi who was a secretary in Germany had problems, but she, too, found work a bit later and worked for a German company, and so they had a good start too.

Both loved it in Canada, and Gunter was for sure not shy speaking English.

One time, we all went to Dairy Queen to get ice cream and Brazier burgers, and without hesitation, Gunter ordered a *brassiere* burger. The person who took the order looked up, and I am sure thought he made a bad joke and asked again. Dietmar apologized for the mistake and explained that the gentleman didn't speak English very well yet, and that, by the way, we were all newcomers, and we were all in the learning process, and so please forgive us. She smiled and answered, "And I thought that he pronounced the word wrong on purpose because he wanted to tease me."

Later when we had our ice cream, and Gunter and Dietmar their Brazier burgers, Die translated to Gunter what happened. We all laughed, and I guess Gunter never forgot, but he was not embarrassed about it at all. Men!

Another time he asked for the washroom to wash his hands. "Where is me washing?" And Dietmar again stepped in and said, "Sorry, he is looking for the washroom." Again, we had our laughs, but sometimes it became a bit embarrassing. (I guess that was my reason for not speaking English; I knew it could come out wrong.) But in principle, he was right, if you don't practice, you don't learn.

Not long after Ushi found work, they moved to Scarborough where they rented a nice, little one-bedroom apartment, and since they were able to walk to work, they saved the fare. We stayed in contact and visited often.

It was at the beginning of November 1962 when we went for a walk. It was miserable outside, and everything looked sad, even the overhanging electric wires above us looked worse on that grey day to us. When we saw the wires, at first, we had to get used to them. In Berlin the infrastructure was different. Even so, Berlin had for the longest time a lot of ruins left from the war; all electrical wires were underground, no overhanging wires anywhere except in the country and on farms.

Dietmar suddenly stopped walking and when I looked up, he had tears in his eyes.

At first, I thought he wasn't feeling well, but he explained that he was homesick and wanted to talk about it. I was puzzled. As a matter of fact, I was shocked and thought I heard wrong. I looked at him with my mouth open, not comprehending what he was talking about because I had no doubt that he was happy here in Canada. And now this?

I looked at him again. "What do you want to do about it, Dietmar?"

"I know, I should be the last one to say it, but maybe you feel the same way that we should go back to Germany?"

I was in shock hearing him saying that—he, who couldn't leave Germany fast enough, wanted to go back!

I looked down at Sabrina who realized that we had an argument going, and turned around.

"Let's go home."

We had our dinner, and after Sabrina was in bed, I interrupted our silence by saying, "Of course, you made a joke earlier, right? You didn't mean it because I can't believe it, simply because you must know that we can't return. We sold everything we had for little money so you could go to Canada as quickly as possible. If we go back, we would have no apartment there and would have to go back on the waiting list. And on top of that, what would your parents or my *Muttchen* say? Or my birth mother for sure, 'We told you so!' I can't believe it, no I can't."

"But Steffie, it came over me because of how often, when I come home, I notice that you were crying, and how often I realized that you and Sabrina were sad. You think I didn't notice?"

"You are right, we both, Biena and I have our moments, but did we ever complain to you, or did I ever say that, for me, it is like being in jail? Because that is the feeling I have when we are alone and wishing the day away because I miss my home. Ours, what we put together, and my family and yours. Yes, it is much better that we have the car and that Sabrina is able to play again or laughs when she is with other children outside. But believe me, I would never ask if we could go back, and to what? As I mentioned earlier, we have nothing to go back to. It's too late. We both agreed to the move, and we have to make the best out of it."

We went to bed that night without closing our eyes and in the morning, Die took me in his arms, and we both cried but knew that we must stick together and make the best out of our grief.

That night after dinner when Sabrina was asleep, we sat down and made a balance sheet, summarizing the 'what' we liked and the 'what' we disliked in Canada and after doing so, we hoped we would be able to conclude what to do: return to Germany or stay in Canada. After we summarized the pros and the cons, we realized that returning to Berlin would be a big mistake, and we both agreed to re-think our situation and future.

The balance sheet showed us that it was no-brainer because after we saw the cons and the pros on paper, it was clear to us that the pros were outweighing the cons and that we had to give it time but maybe make some changes. The first thing was to have our own apartment by moving and to live on our own without the very much appreciated help from the Robinsons.

A few days later, we looked for an apartment and found one in Mimico on Lakeshore Road. It was not the best and was on the ground floor where the windows in the two bedrooms faced the driveway from the parking lot onto the street. So, in the morning it would be noisy. But during the day and at night, it was not too bad, and the rent was the same as we were paying for the rooms we rented from the Robinsons.

Also, we didn't have to sign a lease yet; we could wait until something suitable, on a higher floor, became available.

We moved in on November 30. But prior to that, we had to buy beds and everything we needed for the kitchen, like pots, pans, and dishes etc. because we realized, more than ever, that we had come over with only three suitcases and our little daughter who, by the way, was mighty excited that she would have her own bedroom.

What was strange for us but what we really appreciated was that the kitchen was furnished with a fridge, stove, and cabinets—a luxury that was unknown for us in Germany but, as we learned, here it was standard in apartments.

We bought a TV, another luxury we never would have dreamed of in Germany, and on top of that, we had our own telephone!

Yes, we spent money, but our new home became a cozy little place which was truly our own.

Mr. and Mrs. Robinson were very gracious about our move, and I will never forget them. They knew that our beginning was very hard but, with their help and encouragement, we at least learned to cope with our problems. Not everybody would have had the patience they had with us.

When we told them about our new plans, they wished us luck, and, in a way, we felt close to them. Mrs. Robinson hugged Biena and me and told us that she would miss us. We stayed in contact with them for quite some time. She visited and admired our first house and was so happy for us.

Visit from USA: Uncle Henry 1956

Our wedding-April 6.1957

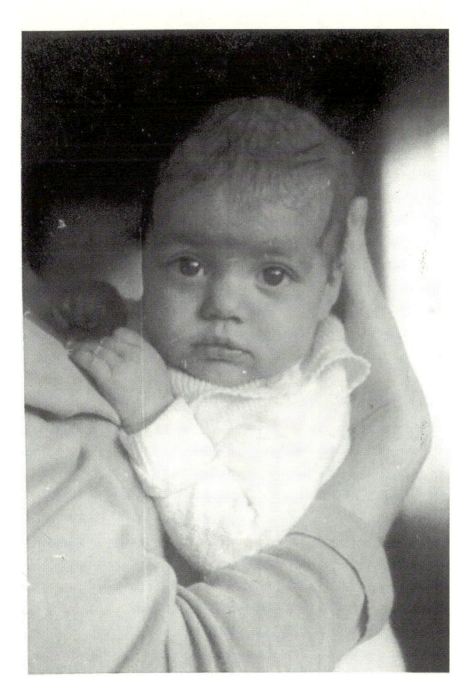

Our daughter Sabrina -December 1958

Proud Papa with his Biena

Mid summer 1960, Sabrina and me, both so happy

Toronto close to High park, where we lived the first 9 Month

Sabrina walked the first time on snow

Our first car in Canada, a 1656 Ford and boy were we proud.

Our first house party in our apartment. We had a ball with all new friends!

Our Son Dean born April 1.1964 after his baptism.
The first Canadian in our family.

Our Chalet- 1977-1987

My Retirement from Heidelberg Canada 1998-1975

New Beginning in Canada

My English improved bit by bit, and I thought that it would be better for all of us if we learned to accept the new surroundings as is: our new home. Sabrina blended in and spoke better English than I. As a matter of fact, at times I had to ask her to speak German, so I could understand what she was talking about.

Our first Christmas in Canada arrived quickly and we thought about "home" a lot and were homesick but, in a way, Biena made it easier for us. She dragged me from store to store and made sure that I helped her with a list for Santa Claus or as she still said, "*Fuer den Weihnachtsmann,*" (for Santa Claus) and "Mami, we need *einen Tannenbaum*" (a Christmas tree).

Our custom in Germany was never having our Christmas tree up before Christmas Eve, but in Canada we learned, trees are up and decorated way before. Back home we had an advent wreath for the four Sundays prior to Christmas Eve. I am sure the Germans still have a wreath. I looked around to find one but couldn't see one, and so two weeks before Christmas Eve, we bought our tree.

Since we needed a small tree, we tried to find one in a lot not too far away from us and looked around, but it wasn't easy. And just when we wanted to go somewhere else, we saw a very small but ugly one. Nevertheless, when we wanted to pass by, somehow, it looked at us and spoke to us, "Take me, please take me!" and Die turned back and said, "Look at this tree, doesn't it look sad, like a Charlie Brown tree? We should take it; it would fit in our apartment, and will give us a good feeling that we didn't ignore it."

Biena grabbed Die's hand, looked up to her father, agreeing, "Yes, Mami, Papa is right, we should take it home, so it has a nice Christmas too."

And so we did; we bought the tree, our first Christmas tree in Canada, and called it our Charlie Brown tree, and in all the years, this tree was never forgotten.

We bought some ornaments and a stand and, even if it was the ugliest tree we had ever had, we loved it.

After the lights were shining on the spruce and the fresh smell carried the Christmas spirit all over our apartment, we were delighted over our choice. (By the way, the electric lights, which were shaped like real candles, were imported from Germany by my favourite bookstore.)

My main occupation during the advent time was to write and send Christmas cards to all our loved ones and friends in Germany.

I remember airmail stamps to Germany were 25 cents, a lot of money for us, but the cards were very cheap, and our friends and family loved receiving our greetings. The custom in Berlin, not like here, was that not everybody received cards. We only sent cards if we weren't able to wish them a Merry Christmas in person. And we sure were not able any longer to take our loved ones in our arms to wish them Merry Christmas any longer, so the cards sent back and forth became very important to us.

I had fun sending these cards, wishing everybody a Merry Christmas, and letting our families and friends know that we were fine and that we liked Canada a lot better than at the beginning of our adventure.

In return, we received parcels and long letters as well, which were put under the tree. We didn't open any presents or letters received before Christmas Eve.

Our presents for Biena and for us were like at home, unwrapped but covered with a blanket, put under the tree until Christmas Eve and only after we came from church were the covers taken off the presents, and parcels from home were visible and unpacked. Dietmar and I had tears in our eyes because we missed all our loved ones, and felt again somehow lonely.

To open the parcels from Germany was a sensation because we were anxious to see what was in them. Dietmar had a tough time with opening them because they were so carefully packed and wrapped so nothing would break. But when everything was finally unwrapped, we were in awe with what was sent to us from overseas. So many sweets, and for Sabrina, clothes and toys. Everything was so special! We couldn't stop hugging and crying happy tears.

It was a wonderful night, and we were happy and knew we would make it in Canada.

Our second winter in Canada was harsh but not so sad and strange anymore. We were much more familiar with our surroundings, and we saw a light in the tunnel.

Dietmar had his second raise and made now $125 per week, and we received a monthly government cheque in the amount of $8, the so-called Child Support for Sabrina. A welcomed small amount because she grew like a weed, and I constantly had to buy new clothes and boots or shoes for her. So, it was a big, unexpected help for us. Our little lady loved receiving new clothes and became a very happy and spoiled little daughter. So spoiled that, at times, I thought she needed a sibling. She needed to know the word "sharing."

One day, the telephone rang. For me, a very strange noise because the only person who ever called was Die.

So when I answered, assuming it was Die, I was surprised to hear a man asking in German if I was Steffie. I was a bit puzzled and asked in return, "*Und wer sind sie?*" (And who are you?).

"Oh, I am sorry, I am Ulli Lada, and I received your phone number from your mother-in-law who is a neighbour of my aunt living in Zehlendorf-Berlin. Your mother-in-law did ask me to contact you and to send good wishes, and so here I am. Maybe my wife and I could get together with you? I'll give you my phone number, and you let me know if and when it would be good for you. I heard so much about you and your husband that it would be very nice to finally meet you."

He talked in German and that alone made my day. I agreed and thanked him for calling and that I or my husband will get in touch with him within a day or so.

When Die came home, and I told him about the phone call, he, too, was excited and called Ulli back that night.

We met shortly after with him and his wife Roseswita and became very quick, good friends.

He told us that he came over in 1957, and as we had, without speaking English. He was a tool and die maker, but there was no work for him because of he didn't know English or French. He worked wherever there was some work, and after three years of hunger and no connections, he was on the brink of giving up. One day, he was so hungry that he stole some food from a store and was picked up by police. After they found out that he was stealing because he was homeless and hungry, they had mercy and referred him to the Salvation Army. The Salvation Army opened their door to him, gave him shelter and food for a week and after, one officer from the Salvation Army gave him an address from a company whose owner was German who was looking for a tool and die maker. He was hired at once and continued working there.

His boss introduced him into the German circle, and there he found his wife, a very young girl whose parents were also German. He laughed saying, "She had just turned sixteen when we got married, and couldn't even go to a bar, married or not, until she turned eighteen."

Germany had different laws and so, again, we realized how much we had to learn.

Shortly after meeting the Lada's, we had another phone call from Harold Podgora.

Dietmar answered the phone, and I heard him saying in German, "Yes, this is him." And after a long pause he answered in German again, "Yes, we lived there before we came over and met your in-laws just shortly before we left. Oh yes, I mentioned to them that we will leave soon to go to Toronto." Toronto, Canada they asked? "My daughter and her husband live there since 1959. I think, in Mississauga, I will give you their phone number, you should get in touch with them."

"Yes," Die said to the person, "they wanted to give us your phone number, but since we didn't see them again, we never got it."

"How did you find us?"

"Oh, I am Harold Podgora as you mentioned you spoke to my in-laws. My wife Lotti found your name in the telephone directory and now here I am, asking if you would like to meet with us."

We met and became good friends. Later the Podgora's moved to the States, but we stayed in contact with Harold's sister Ruth, and her husband Richard.

After a while, we gave our first house party. I bought things from the German deli, all the things I thought German people liked, and later I was proud that everybody enjoyed themselves. So much so that we all were a bit tipsy and by about midnight we had a knock at the door and a policeman was standing there. He came in and saw Richard standing on a chair, imitating Hitler. Even though Richard had never seen Hitler because he was Canadian, he did a good job. Of course, he, too, had one too many and greeted the policeman with *Heil Hitler*, and we couldn't help it; we were laughing ourselves silly. The policeman was a good sport and told us we should stop this game and be quieter because the neighbours complained. Naturally, we complied somehow. The next day we were all a bit embarrassed, but when I think about it now, it was so funny that I still have to laugh about it.

We had a lot of parties. House parties were in but at first, we had only German friends. Later, they were mixed, were noisy, and we always had a lot to drink. Nobody thought twice to drive after a few drinks and very seldom were there ever accidents, because there was not too much traffic? It was not right, but nobody gave it a thought.

Since Dietmar was always sober, he couldn't tolerate alcohol, he was at many times the driver in our circle. Sometimes six or so in one car. Kids and adults had no seatbelts since cars were not equipped with seatbelts yet; Dietmar drove them all.

Good old times, where are they now?

We watched a lot of television because it certainly helped our English.

Sabrina and I liked all the funny shows, but the news was very important to us as well and again, easier to understand than the radio because we saw pictures with the words, and it was faster to observe that way. Like always, the radio was on, too, but one way or the other, we tried to stay informed with what was happening around the world.

Spring arrived and Dietmar came home with a little barbeque, and when he showed it to us and explained what it was used, for I was very skeptical because I never ever knew that most Canadians have one and use it for frying (barbequing) meat, etc. So, we bought hamburger meat, pork chops and corn on the cob, and Dietmar, after he found a nice place outside, close by, started frying, and Sabrina and I couldn't close our mouths watching him.

The charcoal made quite a stink, but a bit later it smelled so good that we couldn't wait to taste the result. Dietmar was in his glory and became quite a chef.

After that, the barbeque was a very important part of our life in Canada. We took the little thing with us to many outings and the smell of charcoal became the sign of a good meal ahead.

When we had company from Germany, Dietmar's mother and, later, his father were always very skeptical at first, but later they, too, loved the taste once they tried it out. They missed it when they went back to Germany and tried to buy one there, but without success. Barbeques were unknown in Germany.

In September 1963, our superintendent phoned us to ask if we were interested in an apartment which was on the second floor, a block closer to the lake. We were, and so a month later, we moved. Again, it was a step forward in our endeavour.

The move only took about two or three hours, and we were settled. The layout was the same, but with a much nicer view because we were just steps away from Lake Ontario, and not to mention, we were away from the noise of the cars rushing back and forth. So nice!

We had nice neighbours there, and Sabrina made new friends. She just started grade one and her English was good, and again, from my point of view, much better than mine. Dietmar and our friends told me that they were surprised at how much I had improved too. People at least could understand what I was talking about.

One day, I saw a babysitting job advertised on Loblaw's billboard, and applied, somehow thinking I wouldn't get it, but I did. It was for a little girl, not even two years old and ever so cute. Her name was Susan, and I think she liked me. Rena, her mother, was happy, too, because she lived not too far away from us, and it was easy for her to bring Susan over in the morning, and her husband would usually pick her up at night.

Little did I know that I was pregnant and a bit later after I took the job, I had to tell Rena about the situation I was in.

She was nice about it but wondered if I could keep Susan at least until she could find another babysitter. I agreed and told her, "I will babysit until I have my baby, which would be by the end of March."

Sabrina and I loved little Susan who had red, curly hair and was so cute and pretty with her beautiful skin that you could just hug her.

Later, after I had Susan already for a while, Rena and I had our laughs when Rena told me that she didn't understand her daughter at times because she spoke German to her.

For instance, I trained her to go to the potty, and so Rena asked me to translate what she was talking about when she needed to go and was picking up her potty. I laughed and said that she hardly needed diapers anymore because she was almost trained and was very proud of herself and her potty.

Her mother was amazed and didn't believe that Susan was potty-trained in such a short time.

"I noticed that she came home without diapers, but I didn't trust the situation and wanted to talk to you about it because I don't understand what she wants at times. "

"Well," I said, "I thought you noticed because she was in training pants during the day, and she very seldom has an accident. I should have told you that we actually can trust her."

We both laughed, and Rena said, "I have to learn German."

Susan soon started repeating so many German words that I was surprised and realized that children learn so much quicker than, for instance, I was. I just hoped that her parents didn't mind. And Rena always assured me saying, "I wish she could stay with you longer and grow up with two languages."

A serious moment came up when, one morning, I had taken Susan shopping, placing her into a shopping cart, and an older man bent over and gave her a compliment saying how pretty she was, and then she answered "Fuck off." I never heard this word before and didn't know what she said to the man but wondered why he just gave me a dirty look and left quickly.

Later that night, Rena called and told me that she couldn't bring Susan anymore since her language was unacceptable, and she repeated to me the same word Susan said to the old man.

I asked her what the word meant and what it was Susan said, "because I have no clue, and I must ask Dietmar to talk to you, maybe he understands and has an explanation. Hold on for a moment I will get him on the phone."

After a while, I heard him laughing, and I had no clue why, and was upset. After they hung up, he told me what the word meant and that we had to find out where she had heard it from, etc. but Rena would bring Susan back next morning.

After we talked to Sabrina about it, we discovered that at her friend's apartment (she lived above us and Sabrina and Susan played there often), the word was used a lot, and so she had picked it up from there.

Die explained to Biena why Susan's mother called and told her never to say this word; it was bad, and we shouldn't talk like that.

"But Papa," she asked, "why is it bad, what is it, because I say it, too, when we play with Sonja. Her mother never told us that it is bad, and we shouldn't say it."

Well, it was hard to explain a word like that to a five-year-old. Die said, "It is a bad word, and I don't want you or little Susan to ever repeat it or say it again." And he continued, "And if you do so, you can't play with Sonja ever again. Do you understand?"

"Yes, Papa, I do!"

Later, when Biena was in bed, I said to Die, "How come they use such words as if it means nothing?"

He answered, "It is the same as when we say 'shit' in Germany. Did you never use that word?"

"Oh, yes, in school, maybe, but not out loud and at home, never. My foster-mother would have for sure given me a long lecture; she never swore."

By the way, Sabrina and Susan played from then on in our apartment with Sonja, rather than going upstairs. At least I could control the "bad" word. But in principle, I hardly understood what these children were talking about. I just saw them playing with toys and pretending to serve tea or something. The bad word was never mentioned in our house again.

In a letter from my mother-in-law, we heard that President Kennedy would be visiting Berlin. She suggested to us to try to see him on television.

We found out that he would be in Berlin in June and, yes, his visit would be televised; we tried but couldn't find the channel.

But I heard him on the radio.

Apparently, there was a crowd of approximately of 120,000 people and in his speech, he gave the Berliners hope they so needed, and they all were beside themselves when he ended his speech by saying, *"Ich bin ein Berliner!"* (I am a Berliner.)

Everyone was so excited and screamed and hugged each other because he assured them that America would be there for them, as they always were when Berlin needed help. They helped West Berliners after the war when they were without water, food or electricity.

And later, when Russia closed the borders, and there was no hope of surviving, guess what? Help came. All three allies again made sure that West Berliners didn't starve like the Russians had planned. Every three minutes, a plane landed to bring food and all the necessities to survive.

The USA and their allies reached out to Germany again, and so the people had new hope with President Kennedy's speech.

When the wall was built to divide the East from the West, Berliners couldn't understand and just asked, "Why?" Many believed a war was imminent and, like us, had very little hope for another resolution.

But the speech gave the Berliners the hope they needed more than ever and like before, they held their heads way up again.

When Dietmar came home that night, we, too, danced for the Berliners. After all, we still were Berliners and proud to be Berliners. We felt the pain, even though we were far away. It was, after all, still our homeland.

Nevertheless, nobody knew at that time that it would be a long, long time before the wall came down. The Berliners learned to live with it and many generations didn't even know the difference at all.

We had a very hot summer, and the kids loved every minute of it.

Dietmar started to get worried about me and told me to look for a good doctor. We didn't have a doctor yet, and all we knew was that we were having a baby.

Talking to Roseswita about it, she laughed and said, "It's about time you see a doctor. Maybe you should try ours. We have one who speaks German and delivers babies as well."

This would be great, at least I could totally understand what he was talking about, and if I had questions, I wouldn't be misunderstood. Yet, I was very nervous and scared to have to go to a hospital and have to speak English. It was a new topic and instead of practicing, my complex appeared again, and I hardly spoke if I didn't have to. Obviously, the baby business was a new subject and not yet included in my English vocabulary. Dietmar understood my problem and, like always, said, "But you can't give up either. As long you understand the person, and vice versa, a bit, nobody will be amused about it or laugh. You will see."

He shook his head, not pleased with me at all, but took me into his arms and asked, "How come you are embarrassed again? You did so well for a short time. Don't give up trying, you will manage just fine."

He let go of me a bit, looked at me with his charming smile, and said, "I can't give up, or do you think it is easy for me? I have to deal with people who speak Italian, Portuguese, Polish and a small group that speaks English, but we all try, and it works. You realize, there is a lot of laughter and that's how to take it. Try and laugh if it comes out wrong and try again. One day you and I will be perfect, mind you, with an accent, but we will be understood, and we will understand."

Soon after Roseswita gave me the phone number of her doctor, I made an appointment with Dr. Pietz, located in Toronto, and I was a bit at ease. All three of us met with him soon after.

He was short with words, and in his way talked very much like, "Come to the point," but was very nice, in general. He realized how nervous I was, but by explaining the whole delivery in Canada, he made it a bit more comfortable for me. He also explained that he would do the delivery and take care of me through the rest of the pregnancy. (At the time, so different from back home, I would have visited my doctor once, and after that, I would have gone maybe once or twice to the hospital where I also would give birth.)

He continued that he would like to see me every month until six weeks prior to the due date, and after, he would like to see me every two weeks or even every week.

"Don't worry, you and I will bring a sweet baby into this world."

The due date was set for March 29, and I mentioned to Dr. Pietz that this was my husband's birthday.

"Dietmar will be so happy about his baby maybe being born on his birthday."

And my Die was. After he heard the date, he was excited and glad that we found this German-speaking doctor. And when we came out of the doctor's office, we both were at ease.

Dietmar took the both of us in his arms and gave us a kiss saying, "So, you see, all worked out just fine and your English and mine will improve, and one day we both will laugh about our complexes."

We prepared for the new arrival and while doing so, we realized that Biena became a bit jealous and unhappy. We were worried about our daughter because, after all, she would be five and a half years older than the baby, and it would be a drastic change for her. She would have to learn to share. We tried to talk to her about the baby quite often, but she always responded by saying, "That is nice, but I don't want one."

I was glad that after the second month of being pregnant, I stopped feeling nauseous and stopped vomiting. Not like with Sabrina, where I didn't stop until the due date. So, I was happy and looked forward to having our second child.

We took advantage of the beautiful summer and went on small trips to learn more about our surroundings. Our friends, Gunter and Ushi, were with us. These friends became very close and the friendship lasted for many, many years.

Sabrina started school in September 1963. She was very young since her birthday is at the beginning of October, but she made the cut to start school very early. She was the youngest in her class but managed just fine, and we were surprised how well she spoke. It always amazed me that children learn so much quicker than adults.

Her attitude towards the baby changed a bit after she went to school full time, I think because she was occupied right from the begin-ning. She liked school very much and she loved learning new things.

Though, using the bathroom in school was another problem. She held on until she made it home (or not). Either she was wet already when she came home or could hold it until she stepped inside our apartment.

When I questioned her, she cried and told me that she was sorry, but the bathrooms in the school were so, so dirty that she would not use them.

After the accidents happened too often, I planned to go to school with her to talk to her teacher.

Me, talking to the teacher? Would she even understand what I had to tell her? Up came my doubts and my complex.

The night before, I hardly slept, and in the morning, I felt nauseous again, but I didn't vomit. Must have been my nerves.

In my mind, I practiced what I needed to say.

Would her teacher understand what I had to tell her?

I wanted Dietmar to come with me, but he couldn't, saying, "I am scheduled for a meeting and can't miss it. You will do just fine by yourself, I know you will."

In the morning, Sabrina noticed that I was nervous and asked if I wasn't feeling well, but I just told her that I would be walking her to school to meet with her teacher and Sabrina asked me why.

I answered, "Not to worry, I just want to talk to her."

The school was not far away from where we lived. With Susan's hand in mine and Biena beside me, we walked as Sabrina did every morning to her school.

We arrived early, but Sabrina's teacher was sitting at her desk already. She looked up at me and asked "Can I help you, Mrs. Steinke?" While Sabrina answered for me, "Miss Sandra, my mommy wants to talk to you, did I do something wrong?"

"Oh no," she said with a smile. "You didn't do anything wrong," and turning back to me, "Mrs. Steinke, why don't we go for a moment out into the hall."

Outside the door, I first of all apologized for my broken English and tried to explain to her my problem. She understood and told me that she was not responsible for the bathrooms, but she would bring it to the principal's attention. I am sure, "he will be able to change the situation. In the meanwhile if it is all right with you, I will talk to Sabrina and will suggest to her to cover the seat with toilet paper before sitting down. Maybe that will help a bit, but again, the bathrooms have to be clean. Thank you for bringing the problem to our attention."

Hallelujah, the teacher understood what I was talking about, and when Sabrina came home she told me the story with the toilet paper and that it helped a bit. "And Mami," she said, "I washed my hands very good too." I was proud of the both of us, her because she could go to the bathroom in school and me because I spoke to the teacher who understood my problem.

From that time on, Sabrina made it just fine using our bathroom without having an accident, but she told me that she still hated to use the bathrooms in school.

I was very happy to have solved the problem and without my husband's help!

One night, after dinner, Dietmar suggested that I should get my driver's licence.

"You will need it soon because going shopping will become a problem if we have a lot of snow on the ground and you have to walk."

I thought for a moment, as I always did when my husband came up with a new idea, that I didn't hear right. How could I get my driver's licence with my English?

Dietmar laughed.

"Simple. I discovered a German drivers' school where all the teachers talk German and since you can read English pretty good, and I believe better than I, you will make out just fine."

"How much will it cost?"

"As far as I know, in a Volkswagen, it is $2.50 per hour, and I am sure we can afford your driver's licence. Let me tell you, it is important that you have it."

"In a Volkswagen? Isn't that with a gearshift, not automatic?"

"Yes, Steffie, you should learn how to drive a car with a gearshift, so you can say 'I am able to drive a car.'"

He smiled, and if I wanted or not, I agreed to give it a try.

"You have to take a written test first and for that, I got you a book you need to study for the rules and regulations. Here it is and now study, and when you think you are ready, you have to make an appointment. I talked to Ulli Lada, and he, after talking to Roseswita, confirmed that she will pick you up to take you where you can take the test and after will bring you back home again. It must be while Sabrina is in school and while Roseswita has a babysitter." (So nice of her, I thought.)

I made an appointment for the following week and got one for Thursday at 9 A.M.

And don't ask me how I did it because it was a wonder for me.

Before I called, I wrote everything on a piece of paper and practiced for hours what I had to know. I also tried to read and learn the content of the book by heart, with my dictionary and without it. It was awful, and I didn't know why I had agreed to all of this.

Thursday arrived, and Roseswita picked me up.

After waiting for quite a while, I was finally called in and had to fill out a form with—I don't know how many questions. At times, I had no clue what they were asking me and after about an hour or so, with my dictionary or with just guessing, returned the paper and prayed that Roseswita was still there, waiting for me. And she was, quite upset, mind you, and asked me what the hell I was doing for so long. "You know, you are the last person to come out of there. At least tell me that you made it."

And I proudly answered, "It was so hard, but yes, I made it."

Dietmar made the arrangement with a German-speaking teacher from the German driving school, and a week later a gentleman knocked at our door, introducing himself as Willy and told me that he was picking me up for my first driving lesson. So far so good!

Willy was a nice man and took the undertaking of teaching me how to drive, not only that but as Die mentioned, in a Volkswagen, which again meant not an automatic but with a standard gearshift. (Dietmar's doing!)

And so it went. Steffie learned how to drive a car.

After Willy explained everything, he drove to a quiet street, and we changed sides and after he explained again and hoped I got it, we were on our way (so he thought) but it was a disaster; however, he was patient, and after I didn't do too many mistakes, he took me to a regular street, and I literally peed my pants. But again, he was a patient man and made sure that I arrived in one piece back home. I trusted him and myself a bit more and agreed to the next lesson a few days later.

When I told Dietmar the whole experience and complained bitterly about the standard gearshift he just laughed and said, "You will see. It is better that way since, later, you will be able to drive any car, not only one with the automatic gearshift." Dietmar didn't have a clue what would follow after I had my fifth lesson. I was sure he didn't think that his wife could ever do something like that.

OK, I didn't either, but a few lessons ahead, Willy came late, and we had to drive in the dark.

I was not really ready to drive in the dark because streetlights bothered me, and I was not happy about the situation, he however insisted because as he said, "There will be a situation when you have to drive at nighttime."

I thought, have it your way, but after a while, he realized how tense I was and told me to relax. "Loosen your hands," he said. "I will take over, nothing will go wrong," and when he tried to help me by loosening up my hand from the steering wheel a little, I bit him.

Boy, did he let go! He stopped the car from his side, and we changed sides. He calmed me down, started laughing and said, "In all my time as a driving teacher, I have never been bitten. You must calm down and trust me or you never will pass the test."

When he walked me up to our apartment, he told Dietmar about the incident, and Dietmar laughed too. "Yes, that's my wife. She is at times terrified and knows how to get out of it by doing something nobody expects."

Willy told Dietmar to practice driving at night with me, but I hardly ever drove at night again.

About three weeks later, I had my test and failed. Apparently, the teacher had a bad leg and due to the weather change was in pain and hardly ever let a person pass, or so Willy told me afterwards.

Four weeks later, I tried again, and this time I had a very young, good-looking instructor. He was very calm and overlooked a lot of mistakes. I had a full bag of candies with me and after a while, we both were eating candies. I lost my fear of making mistakes, and I thought I did pretty well. At least we arrived in one piece at the parking lot. I was pretty sure I did it, and when he asked me and pointed to park the car in the empty space between two cars, I did it without giving it a thought. But after I made it, he continued by saying, "And now back out again and park where there is another empty spot between two other cars, see it? A bit further from here."

I thought I would die but did it again, and was sure I had failed once more. However, he smiled, thanked me for the candies and told me that I just passed the test. I made my driver's licence. And instead of saying thank you, I looked up to the instructor, hugged him and gave him a kiss on his cheek. I think he wasn't used to that but still smiled.

When I saw Willy and told him the good news, he was glad but repeated what he said to me before, to calm down and be careful, and continued, "I tell you one thing, I never will forget you because nobody ever bit me while I gave a driving lesson."

Dietmar gave him a good tip on top of his fee.

Fall arrived with the most beautiful colours we had ever seen, and the weather was very nice and warm. But that changed quickly in mid-October when we suddenly had snow. A lot of it.

I remember, I babysat Roseswita's baby girl that day, and with Susan on my hand, we picked up Sabrina from school when, after a fairly warm morning, the heavy wet snow started to fall.

For me it was so new since we never had snow that early in Berlin.

My worries were that the baby, and Susan and Sabrina coming out of school, were not yet dressed properly for the winter, but no worries, the baby was sleeping, and the kids had fun and didn't even want to go home.

That night, Dietmar came home from work and acted like a little boy. Right away, he promised Sabrina that on the weekend he would take her toboggan to High Park. Of course, the weekend came and the snow had gone. But winter came back soon and, yes, with lots of snow.

We had a harsh winter and it became a bit harder for me to dress the children before we left the apartment.

Sabrina got a new snowsuit (the most practical piece of clothing you could get for the kids here in Canada) and dressed herself quite nicely but with a snowsuit she had a bit of a problem. But little Susan had to be dressed completely, and by the time we were ready to leave, I was covered in sweat. I managed, but we were always happy when we made it and could proceed to go outside.

Christmas is arriving again

By the beginning of November, people prepared for Christmas already, and we were again amazed with how pretty the streets became. The colourful lights lit up the stores and streets, and there were many happy faces; everybody became excited. Canada prepared for a wonderful Christmas season, and so, in a way, we changed our tradition a bit by enjoying the festivity early.

It was our second Christmas in Canada and looking back I can say that we felt more included this time, for sure not as strange as we did when we came.

We asked Sabrina about her wish and what she would like to ask Santa to bring her, and she told us right away, "A Barbie doll but with some clothes, like Sonja has for her doll."

But when I wondered where we could get a doll like she wished for, we received a catalogue from Simpsons (later Sears) plus a letter from the same company in our mailbox, asking if we needed a credit card.

Going through the catalogue, I was amazed at how many products they offered and was happy to see all the wonderful items they had for sale. I didn't need much English to understand what the items were because I saw the pictures and could figure out the description of the article.

In the toy section, I discovered pages of toys and of Barbie dolls. All sorts of them and with the most beautiful clothes to change and dress the dolls.

Still, to phone and order didn't look so easy to me. I wasn't sure if I would be able to manage because whenever a new subject came up,

I had a complex that my English was not good enough and stalled to speak. The application letter was another subject.

We had a credit card from Towers, which was located not too far away from us, and we loved this store. When they offered a credit card, we accepted it not knowing how it works since in Germany we paid for everything in cash. So, after we bought something, and paid with the card, I was amazed at how it worked. Getting a statement and paying the amount they requested was fine, but what I didn't realize was the timeframe. I had no clue that on the balance they (of course) charged interest if you didn't pay by the due date. And so, I was shocked when I looked at the next statement and realized that the amount owing increased instead of decreasing. When Dietmar came home that night, he looked at me and saw that I had been crying.

"What is wrong, are you not well? What can I do, should I call Dr. Pietz?"

But I told him about the statement and asked him to call, "Because if we have to pay *Zinsen* (interest), we don't want the card. We pay cash."

So, he called their office and explained to me that the payment I made was not the full amount and, on top of that, it had arrived two days late, not on the due date; that was why we had to pay the interest. After looking up both words, interest and due date, in my English-German dictionary, I understood the meaning of the words; we didn't use the credit card anymore.

We mentioned the letter to our friend Ulli, who we thought was informed about these things; he laughed and answered straight out, "But you must have credit."

"Why? We don't need the card, and we won't pay *Zinsen*. We have no money for that."

But Ulli didn't give up and explained the process and said, "One day, you might buy a car or even a house; you will need credit for references. So, if I were you, I would get a card from Simpsons; it is, by the way, a well-known and a good card. I would like to mention, too, you never have to pay any interest if you pay the full outstanding balance for that month on due date. If you do that, it is like cash, only you keep it until it is due, almost a month later."

We applied for the card and my first purchase was a Barbie doll and the most important thing, clothes for the doll.

I paid the amount owing punctually and in full and never had to pay interest on credit card charges again.

I loved the catalogues I received regularly. I learned to order on the phone and was pleased to do so and that they understood what I wanted. It was so practical once I was familiar with the sizes, etc.

I used the catalogue a lot and Dietmar was happy about it, too, because he hated to go shopping.

We realized that Canada would become our home one day, and we wouldn't be homesick any longer, but until then, we still were and we missed our family at home.

It was November the 22. I was ironing, and little Susan was playing nicely when suddenly the radio announced a bulletin that President J.F. Kennedy had been shot on his tour in Dallas.

I thought I misunderstood. But, no, I heard right.

Walter Cronkite reported that the president had been transferred to the hospital with shots to his head and was in surgery.

A bit later, Kennedy was pronounced dead, and I think everybody was in disbelief and in deep sadness.

I didn't know much about him but knew that he was in Berlin and the Berliners loved him, which was enough for me to love him too. We knew he was a good man and very much loved by so many people around the world.

The letters from Germany, which followed, told us how much Germany cared for America, and how much President Kennedy was admired and now was missed. I guess many tears were shed.

A visit from the USA

We were having a cup of coffee, enjoying the nice Sunday afternoon when we had a knock at our door.

Dietmar jumped up asking who that could be, and opened the door.

I heard the warm and happy welcome he gave the people at the door, and so Sabrina and I went, too, to see who it was, and recognized Dietmar's aunt and uncle from New York. (I met them in Berlin twice; we were newly engaged, and I was told that they were wealthy.)

Well, what a surprise because Die mentioned to me after we had started dating that he wanted to immigrate to the USA, but when he asked them if they could sponsor him, they declined because he was too young and needed first to finish his education. (But then, I guess, I came into the picture, and he never followed up on the idea.)

When I met them in Berlin, I wondered about the fuss everybody made during their visits, but after they left, Dietmar didn't mention them ever again.

So, it was a surprise to see Uncle Henry and Aunt Hedy standing there in front of our door, and after they came in, they explained how they found us.

Dietmar's mother, who was related to Uncle Henry, told them that we immigrated to Toronto, Canada and since Uncle Henry was in Toronto on business they said, "Here we are!"

It was a very pleasant visit and, I must say, I fell in love with them right away. They seemed to be wonderful warm people.

"You have a cute little place here and a beautiful little Christmas tree."

Obviously, for them, Dietmar made it just fine in Canada, and said, "Our compliments, you should be proud of what you have accomplished in such a short time." (And I knew what Dietmar was thinking: *Yes, and without your help.*)

It was a nice visit, and we were happy that they came.

They stayed in Toronto for three days, and we loved the time we had with them.

They had no children of their own, so they spoiled Sabrina with love and affection right away and us too, by asking Dietmar to drive us all to the Royal York Hotel for dinner.

When we entered the restaurant I was conscious of my clothes because I realized that in principle we didn't fit in, but Dietmar, his Uncle Henry, and Aunty Hedy seemed to like everything, and they didn't care one way or the other. Sabrina was in her glory. She just loved the fuss the waiter made to please us.

They must have reserved a table because at the reception we were treated like special people and were guided to a nice table. Later, the waiter spoke with Aunt Hedy and Uncle Henry as if he knew them.

Uncle Henry explained that before he became semi-retired, he stayed quite often here at the Royal. "But this time it is only for three days to visit you, and what a pleasure this visit is."

We had a fantastic dinner and even Sabrina ate; she didn't complain and behaved like a little lady. We were very proud of her.

A while later, after a wonderful dessert, we said our goodbyes because not only were they tired, but Biena was too.

We left them with the promise to stay in touch and to call and let them know if we ever needed something.

We hugged each other, and Sabrina got a hug and a kiss, too, and we parted.

On our way back home, Dietmar was so excited about the visit, he smiled from cheek to cheek and couldn't stop talking about it.

"Did you notice how pleased they were to see us? Uncle Henry couldn't get enough of Biena."

"Sabrina, did you like them too? They were so nice. Did you like the dinner? Wasn't it something?"

But she wasn't too impressed, and said, "It was OK. I had to go to the bathroom there."

"And Steffie, how did you like the evening? You didn't talk much."

I looked at him. "I was worried about the dress I wore. I wasn't dressed for the occasion; it was a disaster, and I realized I need maternity clothes. I am showing, and it was uncomfortable. Your aunt looked constantly at me."

"No, she didn't, and you looked nice. And don't worry, while you and Sabrina were gone to the bathroom they asked if you are expecting or if you had gained a bit of weight. They remembered you as very, very skinny."

"Ha, ha, so they think I am fat?"

"No, first of all, you are not fat and, secondly, it was years ago that you had met them. Remember the time when they visited Berlin? But I agree, you should buy maternity clothes so you don't look so fat," he teased.

Oh, I could have hit him, but laughed. I knew he joked and loved us and always felt helpless when I or Sabrina was not happy.

At home, he explained to us that we were in the tallest building in Toronto and had dinner in the most expensive hotel.

"Could you write my mother about the visit? They, too, will be happy for us."

Not long after, shortly after Aunt Hedy and Uncle Henry's visit, we received a parcel from Germany and, a bit later, one from New York, but we didn't open them and, even so, Sabrina objected to it; we told her she had to wait until after church on Christmas Eve.

A day before Christmas Eve, another parcel arrived from my foster-mother, and it made me cry, so nice to go through all the trouble, sending us this big parcel. Oh, God, how I missed her. But again, the parcel went right away under the tree until Christmas Eve.

Our second Christmas was a happy one. We went to church, the first time to an all English service, and it was kind of hard for us to follow, but when they sang Silent Night, both of us had tears in our eyes, and we were glad we went and were together with many wonderful people. We listened to so many different languages, but understanding or not, we felt not strange at all in church.

Coming home, I told Dietmar and Sabrina to stay in the hall for a moment.

I rushed to switch on the Christmas lights and to put the rest of the Christmas presents under the tree. It looked all so pretty and festive, and when I asked the two to come and see, they both were excited. We showed Sabrina where her presents were, and she literally ripped the parcels apart and screamed "A Barbie doll, Mami," and a bit later, "and clothes for her, too, oh, *der Weinachtsmann* (Santa Claus) brought all the things I wished for!"

"You were a good girl, and, after all, we think that counts a lot."

"But how does he know? I didn't write anything down because I thought he doesn't understand German."

"Well" Dietmar responded, "I think he reads minds, and he speaks many languages. Next year you write down your wishes, and we will see."

We opened the parcels one by one and in each one we found many sweets, like cookies and candies from Germany, so special for us because, as we remembered, that was always the most important thing under the tree, especially after the war. Sabrina got a doll, and clothes for herself. Nevertheless, the most important thing for her was the Barbie doll and the clothes for her, all she had so hoped to get from Santa.

The parcel from New York had mostly clothes for both her and the baby. Everything was so nicely wrapped in Christmas paper, which was admired more than what was in the packages. We were not very familiar with wrapping paper because, again, after the war, there was none to have, and so for us, it was rich to receive everything so nicely wrapped.

We had to get familiar with the Christmas customs here in Canada; they sure were different from back home, but we enjoyed every bit of it. Yes, we missed our family, but our second Christmas in Canada was better than the year before, and we were sure that the next one would be even better because we would have our baby by then.

Right after the New Year, I bought nice maternity clothes, and I didn't look too pregnant yet. Dr. Pietz was pleased that I hadn't gained too much weight and assured me that everything was fine. "Good," he said. "It's so much better if you don't gain too much weight. You are just fine the way you are. I like it; when the time comes it will help the both of us to deliver that baby. Believe me, you will gain a bit more and that's OK. Your baby has a nice cradle. Don't worry!"

I thought he was funny, but it stopped me from worrying. After all, I had three full months to go.

We had bought a crib and a little chest for the baby and placed it in Sabrina's bedroom, but she was upset.

"Mami," she cried, "I don't want the baby furniture in my room; it can sleep in your room."

Well, it took both of us to calm her down and to convince her that it is right to share the room with the baby, and I said, "I will always take it out of your room when it cries, so it will not disturb you a bit. Let's wait first and see."

She was not impressed, but she stopped crying.

I didn't know where the time went, but between babysitting Susan and looking after Sabrina, it sure went fast, and suddenly my stomach grew quite a lot. I carried the baby all around and, therefore, was not showing as much as I had with Biena.

Sabrina told her father that I was fat. And he should tell me to stop eating so much because she didn't like me being fat.

Dietmar laughed and said, "Why don't you tell her yourself?"

"No, she will be angry or sad. I don't know, but you tell her. I don't want to get in trouble."

Of course, I overheard the whole conversation and had to laugh, too, but said, "You will see, once the baby is here, I will be skinny again."

We practically had to stop her and get off the subject, but we realized that she didn't understand the process and that we had to talk to her.

A few days later I started by saying, "You want to feel the baby when it moves?"

And she looked at me and asked, "Why, where is it, in your tummy?"

"Yes, that's why I am fat right now," and suddenly I realized that we missed telling her sooner that we were expecting a baby that I carried in my stomach.

After she touched my stomach, she got excited, and the baby was not a problem any longer. (We hoped.)

She wanted a little sister and couldn't understand that we had to take whatever we would get, and further, she wanted to know how it got in there, but I backed out and told her I would explain to her later. She let it go, but I was sure that, somehow, Dietmar and I would have to face the fact and that she would come back with further questions.

We went to Toronto to visit the auto show. I guess it was by the end of February, the beginning of March, and while walking from one dealership to the next I realized that I lost some fluid. Dietmar was not too worried about it at all, but asked, "Are you in pain?" and when I said "no," he told me to sit down and took Sabrina by her hand and walked on.

We later went home, and I had no further problems. But I was mad at him; it was like he cared about the cars more than his wife. When I mentioned it to him, he reminded me that I had the same problem with Biena, and so he wasn't worried too much. "By the way, if you had been in labour, we were in Toronto, not too far away from North Western Hospital, so again, I was not worried at all."

Three weeks later, we had a terrible snowstorm, and Dietmar called from work to tell me that he wouldn't make it home and, further, that he was going to stay with a colleague for the night. I panicked and cried, but again, he stayed calm and said, "Nothing will happen! But in case, should the baby decide to come, call Ulli; he knows what to do. I talked to them about it already, and they assured me not to worry. They will help." He also said, "I am sorry, Steffie, but I can't make it, and I am sure you don't want me to be in an accident."

And he was right, the baby didn't come.

March 29, 1964, my due date and Dietmar's birthday! But nothing happened either!

Well, we had lots of snow on the ground, but we went to Pickin Chicken BBQ, a place on Lakeshore Boulevard in Mimico for Die's birthday. Sabrina thought it was cool to have dinner in a restaurant for her father's birthday, which was a cheap family restaurant, but the food was good, and we all were happy.

I became a bit anxious and all around big, and generally uncomfortable, but other than that we were good.

I bought a nice birthday cake from the German deli, and since it was a Sunday, we had plenty of time to continue the small celebration at home, and I was glad that my husband enjoyed his day.

The night was quiet, too, because absolutely nothing happened.

I wished it would start but no, no signs. The baby was obviously comfortable and in no hurry.

The next morning, Rena brought Susan and told me that if I needed to go to the hospital to call her right away; she would pick Susan up without delay. She said that she had spoken to her supervisor already so everything would be under control. "I wish that you would have the baby soon because you look like it will pop out any minute." We both laughed.

Sabrina came back from school. Rena picked up Susan, and I still hobbled around.

I saw Dr. Pietz on Friday of last week, and as he said, everything looked like a go! He told me that the baby was not a small one, "But you, yourself, didn't gain too much weight, which is good! So, I am sure I will see you next week in the hospital."

I mentioned castor oil because back home when I had Sabrina, they finally, after twenty-seven hours, gave it to me, and it helped.

Dr. Pietz kind of smiled but didn't say anything, except he shook his head, and I heard him whispering. Typical Germans.

On Tuesday, again nothing. I babysat Susan and while she had her nap, I thought I was bit overdue, so why not…and took, after Biena came back from school and Susan was picked up, a teaspoon of castor oil. What a taste, but at least hopefully I could get to the bathroom because maybe that was why I was so uncomfortable.

Dietmar came home and the first thing was like always, "How are you?"

"Oh, I am fine, and how are you, how was your day?"

"Good too. By the way, the women at work always ask me how you are making out, and Martha, a German girl, mentioned that you should take castor oil, but only if you are over the due date and if the baby is in the right position. She said it helps a bit with bringing on the contractions."

Now I laughed and confessed that I had just swallowed the awful stuff, and we would see what would happen. I knew for sure it would help me to go to the washroom.

I was tired that night and went to bed early, way before Sabrina and Dietmar did, but woke up by eleven to go to the washroom. Pretty normal by the way, but when I wanted to go back to bed I had a slight contraction, which I had before, so I wasn't too excited.

By twelve, I had one again, and after, about every fifteen minutes, and I knew I was starting to go into labour.

I woke up Die, and he phoned the Ladas to say that we would be bringing Sabrina over soon and Rena as well, that she shouldn't bring Susan in the morning.

I went to take a shower, and Dietmar looked after Sabrina, and by three we were on our way, first to Lada's and afterwards to the hospital.

About fifteen minutes before our arrival at the hospital, we had to pass train tracks, and Die sped in order to make it before the gates came down. We heard the warning single already and made it all right, but we had the police behind us and on top of that, I noticed that my water had broken. Dietmar had to stop because the police sirens came on.

The officer, a young man, asked what the rush was because Dietmar should have stopped at the pass, and Dietmar's answer was, "Sorry, officer, we are having a baby, my wife's water just broke, and she has contractions about every 10 minutes."

"Oh," he answered. "I think, in that case, I won't give you a ticket, and you had better follow me or you will get a ticket for sure with the speed you are driving. Is it North Western Hospital?"

"Yes, I think," he queried, "it is not too far away from here?"

"No," he laughed. "It isn't, but it is better we speed together."

We were there in no time, and I was looked after at once. Dietmar was told to wait outside or to go home (in 1964 husbands or relatives were not allowed to be in the delivery room), "Because your wife has for sure another 4 to 5 hours before the baby will be born."

And so it was. Dietmar went home, and I was by myself.

As I understood, Dr. Pietz was not even called yet, but who was I to know what was right or wrong?

A nurse came in and checked everything and confirmed that we had plenty of time.

After she left, I dozed off a bit and woke up with a terrible contraction and called the nurse, but she said, "No worries, everything looks fine," and she left.

She was out of the door when I had such a pain that I called her back.

She came, not impressed with me, but I asked her to have another look.

"This is my second baby, and I am sure you should check again," and I continued with asking her if she had children of her own, which she denied.

I said very desperately, "Check again!"

She did and yelled, "Don't push. I need to call the doctor."

She folded my legs and left in a hurry and about fifteen minutes later, which were agony for me, Dr. Pietz came in and had a look. He smiled saying, "That's my girl. Now you can push; I will help. It will not be long before we will have the baby."

To push was a joke because I was in agony from not being allowed to push yet but when I did push, it was like something exploded in my head. I screamed for Dietmar, for my *Muttchen*, for anybody and swore saying, "Oh shit, oh shit," but all I heard was Dr. Pietz saying, "Come on, Steffie, you can do it. We are almost there." And again, and again, "Push!" I did and a bit later, I felt like my whole body had exploded, and the doctor said, "That's my girl, here we are," and I heard the loud scream, not from me, but from a baby, my baby—I did it!

Dr. Pietz said very happily, "It's a boy, and he is healthy and very loud already. Congratulations, you did wonderfully."

It took altogether approximately one hour, and we had a baby boy. He weighed exactly eight pounds and screamed from the top of his lungs.

After he was cleaned up, they showed me my baby for a moment and put him on my chest. What a wonderful baby and so cute already. But not long after the nurse came, took him and told me he would be in the nursery. I was looked after, too, but after a short observation, they kept me in the room because I didn't feel well and shivered badly. I was not able to stop, and they called Dr. Pietz back.

"What are you doing to me? All is over, and you were a trooper, and now you shiver? You are in a bit of shock, and we will fix that." He gave me a needle and left saying, "I will see you after you are in your room."

I calmed down a bit, had even a little snooze, but it took almost one hour before the medication calmed me down completely, and I was wheeled into a room with only two beds, but the bed beside me was empty.

I was so surprised because in Germany nobody could afford a private or semi-private room. So I asked, and they didn't know what I was complaining about. They assured me that our insurance was paying for it, and I didn't have to worry about it at all.

Dietmar came about an hour later with a little wilted rose bouquet and was also absolutely a mess. He couldn't believe that we had a boy, all healthy, cute and so quick to come out. After he saw his little boy, he soon left because he had to go to work but promised to come back later. I was worried about Sabrina, but he assured me she was looked after and so said again that he would see me again right after work.

"Relax," Dr. Pietz told me, "you were a trooper, and I love you!"

Before Dietmar wanted to leave, Dr. Pietz checked in, and they talked for a moment. He told him that he was very pleasant and assured us both that the delivery of that beautiful little boy was absolutely perfect.

He looked at me and said, "She did a good job," and to Dietmar, "I heard you went home instead of waiting outside."

"Yes," I answered for Dietmar, "we thought for sure that I would have the baby much later because, as we told you, it took me with our daughter altogether twenty-seven hours."

He laughed and joked by saying, "Only in Canada or castor oil (?). You realize, it sure was fast."

"I know," blushing, realizing what he meant and answered, "Never."

By afternoon, I wanted to see my little boy. I didn't see my baby much after giving birth, and because I didn't nurse, I had to go to the nursing room to be able to see him.

I asked the nurse on duty, and she offered to help me to walk over. It was not far and, "If you feel up to it, I will come back in about an hour to help you up." And as promised, we walked, slow, but with her help it was not bad at all.

He was placed in the middle of two cute-looking babies, and I didn't recognize him at first. He looked different, I thought, and I had to ask the nurse which baby was mine. She laughed and explained it was probably because he was placed in the middle of two Italian-background, sweet-looking baby girls. "Babies born by parents coming from around the Mediterranean look a bit older and very cute because they already have that mature look," she joked. I thought our baby was perfect too and the cutest of them all. He, too, had beautiful big eyes and black hair, but not as much as the babies beside him.

Dietmar was ecstatic when he saw him early in the morning. He told me that he was beautiful like his sister was when she was born.

We were so thankful that our son was healthy and the first Canadian in our family.

When Die came back later, right after work, he was beside himself and so absolutely happy, but apologized for the not-very-fresh roses he gave me in the morning. He explained that he bought them from an outside machine since the store was still closed. He gave me a kiss and whispered in my ear, "But I bought you something else. I hope you like it," and gave me a nicely wrapped little package.

I was very excited and in a hurry to see what it was and unwrapped it quickly. I could hardly speak and had tears in my eyes when I saw what he had bought for me. It was a golden bracelet with a little baby shoe charm on it, so absolutely beautiful and sweet. Only Die could find something so special for me. He was glad that I had forgiven him for the wilted roses, which I thought was a wonder that he had even found flowers so early in the morning, and I told him that I was happy, one way or another.

Dr. Pietz came back in the afternoon to look at me, checking how I was doing when he saw the little box I had on my night table.

"Ah, a present again?"

I showed it to him, and he said, "That's more like it because the roses didn't look too good for a wonderful little baby boy like you have."

He was always joking, which surprised me because when we met the first time, he didn't seem funny at all.

During the night, another very young, small-built girl was placed in the empty bed beside me.

She was noisy; she whimpered a lot and told me that she delivered a girl, weighing over ten pounds, and she ripped and had a cut and stitches from one end to the other. No wonder she was in pain.

I asked her who delivered her baby, and she answered, "Dr. Pietz."

"He is upset with me because I didn't listen to him when he warned me about my eating habits. He wanted a smaller baby, closer to six pounds rather than ten pounds. He did warn me several times and put me on a diet, but I didn't listen."

"Well, I guess you should have listened."

The next day, Dr. Pietz told me that I could go home tomorrow, and I was pleased because in Germany I had to stay a whole week.

In Berlin, 1958 when I had Sabrina, hospitals didn't have semi or private rooms, and the delivery room had no curtains nor any privacy whatsoever. Most of the time, there were up to five women in the delivery room, whimpering or screaming, and we had midwives, no doctors. A doctor was only called if there was an emergency. But it was not long after the war, and so different and surprising for a newcomer.

We have a son!

Dietmar picked us up and brought Sabrina with him and when she saw her brother the first time, she was happy too. She looked at him, bent down and gave him a little kiss. So sweet, Dietmar and I were glad. We somehow expected more resentment, but there was none.

On our way home Biena asked for the name, and we both laughed. In the hospital, we thought about calling him Dean, but we were not sure and asked her, "You like the name Dean?" And she answered, "Yes, it's a nice name." And so, Dean it was.

We arrived home without a problem and I, with Dietmar and Sabrina beside me, put Dean in his new crib.

I had bought and sanitized bottles, etc. But no formula.

Again, it was all different when I had Biena, and I had to learn again, not only to diaper him because we, in Germany, never used pins, and now diapering made me nervous. I needed to do it correctly without hurting the baby.

I had plenty of baby clothes mostly sent from Germany, different from here, but nice too, and so when we came home, my concern was only the formula.

I learned much from Roseswita since she didn't nurse either, and in the hospital, I was told to try the formula Enfalac. They gave me a little sample, maybe for two servings, and I prepared a bottle but asked Dietmar to get more formula and more bottles.

Dietmar, with Sabrina on his hand, went to the drugstore and bought Enfalac. The formula came in tins so he bought two which was almost too much because I didn't know yet if the baby liked it. He also bought the bottles since I was told I could prepare two or three bottles at once and keep them in the fridge, which was convenient for the night feedings.

How different it was with Sabrina. Because we had no fridge, we had to prepare a new bottle every time, regardless of where we were. The preparation was tedious and a pain. I learned to do it quickly and later had no problem, but as I said, here in Canada, I realized soon, it is all so much easier and faster.

By the time Dietmar and Biena returned, Dean was crying to tell us that he was hungry, with a voice I remembered from Biena. I diapered him and had problems with the pins, but after trying a few times, I did the job and was thankful that my two helpers came home with formula and that I could prepare more bottles for him.

Surprisingly, he drank his three ounces, burped, and by the time I put him back into his crib, he was already asleep.

Dietmar went out again to get some chicken for dinner, and we all settled down a bit.

The night was different. With every little noise I heard, I jumped right away to make sure that Dean was OK and didn't wake up Sabrina nor Dietmar because Dietmar had to go to work and Sabrina, to school.

It was a huge difference with a baby and started at once, with the very first night. Yes we knew, after all, we had Sabrina, but it felt all new with so many years between the two of them. We were in another country, now with two children and surrounded by sometimes to us strange customs, and without relatives. Yet, we didn't mind and felt that we belonged here because we had a little Canadian in our family and were proud about it.

I fed Dean twice during the night, and both Sabrina and Dietmar were surprised that they didn't hear a peep. Needless to say, I was like all new mothers, exhausted, but life went on, and I learned quickly to cope.

The next day I established a little routine and somehow it worked. Both Dietmar and Sabrina were astounded that the baby always slept through, until the next weekend when Dietmar woke me up in the middle of the night to tell me, very upset, that his baby son screamed, as he said, very loud, "Don't you hear it? He must be hungry."

"Yes, probably he is. What time is it?"

"About midnight."

"That is the time he gets hungry; after all, he slept for three hours and that's good."

So Dietmar brought the baby, holding him ever so carefully and wanted to go back to bed, but I took Dean, cradled him and asked Dietmar to heat up a bottle, which as he knew was in the fridge.

"Heat up the bottle, how?"

"Well, you watched me last night and all you have to do is put the bottle in hot water until it is warm. I will change him in the meanwhile."

He heated up the bottle as I told him, but that was it, because he became so nervous even doing that, he broke out in heatwaves, his pyjamas were soaked in sweat.

Dietmar stayed up and watched the whole procedure and was amazed at how much work there was to comfort our little guy, but I think he was afraid of hurting the baby, even changing the diapers.

I explained, for the time being, this was the night routine, and I wished that he could at least help me on weekends.

He agreed, but it was wishful thinking on my side because Dietmar was simply too scared to even hold his son, and said, "I might break him," and refused to give him the bottle.

He promised to help with anything else, but not with the baby, repeating again, "I might hurt him." (I guess times changed.)

And so it was and as I remembered, he was the same with Biena. Only after she became older, he practically took over, by playing with her and entertaining her, but never changed diapers nor fed her at an early stage of her little life.

A few days later, we ordered a baby carriage from Sears. It was delivered during the week and had to be assembled, and since I was, as always, very impatient and couldn't wait, I did it myself and was very proud to show Dietmar, after he came home from work, the fully assembled carriage.

He checked every little screw and had to admit that I had done it properly, but all he said was, "My wife can't wait! And don't complain that it was a hard job to do because you shouldn't have it done in the first place."

Dean, by the way, liked the carriage, and so did I because during the day but mostly during the night, he slept in there, and it was so much better for me. I was always close to him, and I was not nervous anymore that he might cry and wake up Dietmar or Sabrina because I pushed the carriage out of the room to diaper and feed him.

Ladas were the first visitors and admired the baby. They brought a little toy for him, and it was appreciated. We had more visitors who brought little presents for Dean but there was never anything for Sabrina, and I realized soon she was sad about it and felt left out.

In time, parcels from Germany arrived, and with the more we received, the more she became upset. She was so upset that one day she took all the presents and threw them into Dean's crib, almost right on him; she could have killed him. I was in the bathroom, and when I came out, I realized what had happened. Dean was crying, and I screamed at her, "Stop it, stop it!" But she screamed back, "I hate him! He gets so many presents, and I get nothing."

After I checked the baby and was glad that he was not hurt, I took her and cradled her and told her that I was sorry and promised that we would go shopping on the weekend and buy something for her, something she really wanted. "Maybe a toy or a new dress?" I suggested. Her tears disappeared and right away, she told me that her Barbie needed some new clothes. And further, "Please don't tell Papa, please Mami, I am so sorry for what I did."

I promised that I will not tell and hugged her, but also warned her, "Don't do it ever again. It was not his fault, and you could have hurt him."

When Dietmar came home and asked us how our day was, we both said, "Fine." Yet Sabrina was somehow a bit different to her father, she hugged him a lot and was constantly around him, I guess he didn't notice but later when she was asleep, I told him about the incident and said right away that it was our fault, not our friends' and family's fault. We should have thought about Sabrina and given her little presents as well. Remember in Germany, nobody brought presents for a new baby in the first place; they came to congratulate us on the new arrival. So OK, we had no idea that it would hurt Biena.

"I am not mad at her at all, and told her not to cry or be mad at her baby brother and that she will get a present as well. I feel sorry for her; after all, she is still a little child too."

Another lesson learned, to adjust to Canadian customs.

The weather was not bad for April, and I took Dean out almost every day to either pick up Biena from school or to walk to Lakeshore, mind you, very proudly with my carriage and our beautiful baby boy.

The fresh air was good for the both of us, and I enjoyed walking. He was a good baby and cried only when he was wet or hungry. Mostly hungry, but I always changed him, probably too often. I was afraid that he would get a rash. The diapers were not like they are today. But I boiled them every day, as I had with Sabrina's; it was quite a job, but I didn't mind because I knew they were almost sterile.

I found out that there was a diaper service available, but I knew how it was handled. I worked in Germany in an office for a large laundry company and, therefore, knew all about it: and I guess here, too, the laundry was placed in ten separate compartments, yet washed with the same water. Mind you, the diapers came out clean but smelled very strongly of bleach. So, diaper service was out of the question for me. Not in Germany nor in Canada.

My mother-in-law came for her second visit in mid-July, and we had a wonderful time with her. She was beside herself when she met her little grandson, but for her, Sabrina was still her darling first grandchild, and I was told, she was until *Oma* died.

We all had a great time with Mother, and Dietmar took us all over the place, even to Algonquin Park.

We started the trip with the knowledge that it would be a long trip and left at 5 in the morning.

Mutti or *Oma*, as we called her, wanted to sit at the window in the back with Dean, in his carriage bed, and Sabrina beside him. Of course, there were no baby seats yet, not even thought off.

On our way, we took many rests since *Oma* had to pee. She smoked a lot. Everything went fine until without our knowledge, *Oma* didn't put out her last bit of her cigarette and took it with her into the car. We were shortly on our way when I, and a second later, Biena smelled something burning and told Dietmar to stop the car. We got out and found a bit of ash from the butt on the inside of Dean's carriage bed. It had melted the interior of the carriage already.

I was beside myself. Die started screaming at her and woke up the baby, and Sabrina cried, but stroked her *Oma*'s cheeks, telling her not to worry because nobody got hurt.

We all were even more upset when *Oma* held the rest of the butt between her fingers and wanted to throw it out onto the ground in the middle of the forest. Dietmar almost lost it.

"Do you know what you wanted to do, just now after the damage you did before?" he asked. "It's not enough that you almost burned the baby and ruined the bed of the carriage, and on top you wanted to start a forest fire as well?"

At that point, I didn't want to be involved in the fight. I stepped out of the car, took the butt and made sure it was completely out, even putting a bit of water on it.

After we all cooled down, she apologized and said, "It never will happen again." She was very upset with herself and repeated that she didn't know what she was thinking. "It could have hurt the baby or started a forest fire and, as Dietmar said, I have no excuse for that but only to beg you, please forgive me. PLEASE!"

We stood there for a while before we continued our trip, but we forgave her and, I must say, the rest of her holidays were nice.

Algonquin Park is a beautiful place, and one has to admire the landscape. Many told us that it is even prettier in the fall, but we were excited to see it as it was in mid-summer.

After our encounter with mother, and we calmed down, we found a restaurant, had a nice dinner, and I was able to look properly after Dean. We made it home by about 10 at night and were all very, very tired.

Dean slept until after 4 in the morning and the rest of the family was up by 8.

Since Dietmar was on some holidays, we were not in a rush after the long trip the day before, and went down to sit at the beach of Lake Ontario.

Oma apologized again, but Die told his mother to stop it and forget it and took her in his arms.

"What's done is done," and as Biena said, "We all are happy that nobody got hurt."

We went on several other trips and before we realized it, Dietmar's mother had to fly back home. At the airport, we all cried and hugged because we knew that it would be a while before we would see each other again, after all, it was a long distance between us and many letters away.

Shortly after Dietmar's mother left, we had Dean baptized. We realized that we should have done it while Mutti was with us, but the timing was wrong.

The service was done by the pastor who picked us up from the airport when we arrived in Canada. It was a wonderful service, and after, we drove back to our apartment. We had no party or even a dinner, like we would have had in Germany, but we had each other and two healthy children and were very thankful for that. Yes, we missed our family, but we were happy. Dean grew so quickly, and both children gave us much joy.

It was fall when Dietmar's uncle and aunt phoned to say that they wanted to visit us, but mainly to see the baby since they hadn't met him yet.

Uncle Henry mentioned that they would be thankful if we could find a nice hotel close by because they had no other plans other than to see us and said, " Don't make a fuss. We will have most dinners in a restaurant, and again, no fuss, please!"

Dietmar found a hotel not too far away on Lakeshore in Mimico, and we hoped it was sufficient and 'fine' enough for them. Later, they assured us that everything was great.

Dietmar had some holidays outstanding, so he had time to drive them around if they wished so and to entertain them a bit.

But as we learned, for them, the children were the most important reason to visit, and they couldn't see enough of both. They were surprised about Sabrina, at how much she grew and admired Dean for how cute and quiet he was. Uncle Henry, in particular, watched me when I gave Dean a bath and dressed him or changed his diapers. I felt that he still missed having children of his own.

I think we had a good time together. I cooked quite a lot and prepared nice meals for us, and they assured me that they liked my cooking.

They always wanted to know how we coped and were surprised and commented that my English wasn't too bad at all. And again, they loved the children.

They had a niece, who was, for them, more like their own child than a niece, but, she was an adult now, a professor, and taught at the university in New York.

Shortly before their departure, Uncle Henry asked us how we were making out financially, and if they could help with anything. But we told him that we were fine and that we were saving for a down payment for a house.

Die told him that we were looking for a house and concluded that we would rather buy a new house than an older one, because in the long run it would be probably less expensive. Houses we saw all needed costly renovations. And on top of that, Steffie is so very sensitive to smells and the older houses all somehow smelled. They laughed, but Aunt Hedy agreed with me because, I guessed, she was sensitive to smells as well.

Later, after Dietmar returned from taking them to their hotel, he told me that his uncle offered to lend us $500 over five years without interest. As he said to Dietmar, he noted that we didn't have the amount for the whole down payment together yet, and he thought it might help us fulfill our goal a bit quicker.

"Think about it, Steffie," he said after a pause. "It is a great offer. I know you don't like debt, but isn't that be the best offer we ever have received?"

"Did you agree already?"

"No, you know I wouldn't dare to do so without talking first to you, my"—as he always called me—"fiance minister." We both laughed. (To him, I was always his finance minister because he couldn't care less about money.)

"So, we can wait with our answer, and I can make a budget first before we commit?"

"Oh yes, remember this is a favour; he wouldn't make any money on that; he only suggested it to help us."

"You put your budget together, including all expenses, making sure we could afford the monthly mortgage payments plus living expenses, and if we can afford to buy a house, we will let him know."

And so, on the day they came to say goodbye and before Dietmar drove them to the airport, we told them how great it was of them to lend us the money and that we would love to accept the help to buy our first house.

"It is a dream come true, and we never could have done it so soon without help. Thank you so much for helping us."

Both Uncle Henry and Aunt Hedy were so happy and assured us that they were glad to help. Uncle Henry finished the conversation by saying, "Let us know when you need the money."

Their departure was somehow sad because during their second visit, we got to know them and, in a way, they became family to us.

Shortly before they went home, Uncle Henry talked a bit about his immigration to the U.S.

He, too, had a hard time at first because it was a few years after World War I had ended, and since he didn't speak a word of English, it was not easy for him as well.

His uncle had been in America for years and was very much settled, but had no family and sponsored Henry to come to America. Hedy followed a year later, and they lived right away in very wealthy surroundings. His uncle, along with a partner were the co-founders of Wrigley's, the maker of chewing gum, and where Henry started to work right away. After he was able to speak fairly good English, he became manager of sales for Germany and later, vice-president of sales for USA.

Before moving to their apartment on Park Avenue, they lived for quite some time in a four-room suite in Bristol Hotel and Aunt Hedy never worked in her life. She told me that she loved cooking, but they always had somebody to help and clean up afterwards. They both had a very good start and were spoiled right away, but yet, they were good to be with because Uncle Henry was very much down to earth.

They tried to have children, but it didn't work for them, and so they gave up on the idea. They told us they would have loved to have had children of their own, but that explained why they sure loved ours so much.

A house for us?

A week after his uncle and aunt left, we started seriously looking for a house again because we figured, with our saved money and the loan, we had the down payment.

It took us about four weekends before we found a house we liked, located in Clarkson on Truscott Drive.

It was a bungalow with three bedrooms, a big bathroom, all electric heating, and a nice-sized basement, and since it was a model home, we could move in on January 15, 1965.

After putting all the details together, we made a new budget. We wanted to make sure that we could pay the monthly mortgage payments plus living expenses etc., in other words, that we would be able to afford the house and still live comfortably.

What we hadn't considered was that we needed furniture since we had almost nothing in our apartment. So again, before we signed papers, we asked if it was possible to pay less down, and were told that this was not possible, but maybe a second mortgage would help. I said right away, "NO," but the salesman didn't give up that fast and put a plan together, which didn't look too bad at all. The second mortgage would only be for three years and must be renewed or paid out on the due date.

We went back home, again, without signing anything. The salesman very patiently suggested that we get a lawyer and talk to him before signing anything.

"A lawyer?" I asked. "How much will that be?"

He ignored my question, but said, "As I suggested to you before, you need a lawyer for the purchase. I do understand your worries. It is hard to buy your first house, and it is very smart to investigate everything prior to the purchase, but in the long run, you will need a lawyer, not only to understand the procedure but to make the papers you will have to sign legal. I am sure you will be fine."

We went home, and we both saw our dream crumble.

We had nobody to ask and didn't want to bother Uncle Henry at all, and thought the best thing was to postpone the whole idea until we were sure we could cope without being too tight with our money.

Dietmar, however, looked for and found a lawyer, one who spoke German and was located close by as well, and made an appointment.

"It can't be all that expensive and maybe it opens the door we just closed."

And so, we met with a lawyer. I guess, for both of us, it was a first.

As I mentioned, he was located in Clarkson, not too far from where we wanted to purchase the house, and as we thought, the most beautiful house on the planet.

The Wolfs babysat for us, and Dietmar picked me up after he came home from work to visit "our" lawyer.

Entering the offices, I said right away that the office looked too plush for us and it seemed that he might be very expensive.

Dietmar laughed and whispered, "You and your money; we will make it, you will see. Having you watching over our money like a hawk, we will never overspend our budget, and I know that we will have the house soon."

While waiting for a moment in the waiting room, Dietmar was calm and collected, and I was nervous like a tiger in a cage.

A bit later, a secretary asked us to follow her and guided us to the office of Mr. Kutcher, a very good-looking, middle-aged man who greeted us in German and asked us to sit down. His secretary offered coffee or tea, which we declined, and he asked us what he could do for us.

We talked about our plans and the second mortgage, my most important worry.

We stayed with him for half an hour and left much happier than when we were coming. Driving home, we both understood all the ins and outs and were sure we could manage the second mortgage if we cut down with small things, like going out for dinner at times.

The following weekend, we went back and signed the deal, and a few days later we were proud owners of a small but nice bungalow, and had possession on January 15, my birthday.

We bought furniture for every room, especially for the children, and Dietmar repainted one wall in both of their rooms in a different colour. Sabrina thought that that was very special.

We bought a wringer washing machine, but no dryer; we had a large basement, and I could hang the clothes inside or outside to dry.

Yes, we had the second mortgage, but we put half of it in the bank, planning to pay it all off ASAP. It still gave me the creeps, but at the moment it sure helped. We didn't mention it to Uncle Henry and Aunt Hedy.

After we were finished with decorating, moving in and pushing furniture back and forth to find the right spot, we were so proud that, with the help of Uncle Henry, we accomplished everything in a shorter time than we could have ever hoped for. Canada not only gave us more than we had expected, but it gave us the freedom we believed we could never have had in Germany.

The wall, which divided the country, was so very high and sad, but we always heard the Germans, especially the Berliners, were tough and coped with it. Remembering the time during and after the war, I think there was a lot of truth to it.

We, here in Canada, missed our homeland a lot, but we chose to make Canada our home, we just had to give it a bit of time!

After the move in the winter on an especially cold day, we received our first electricity invoice of $50, and I almost fainted! Right away I called Dietmar and told him that we had to sell the house again because that was never included in our budget.

Dietmar couldn't talk much on the phone but said, "We will talk about it later. Don't forget how cold it was on our moving day, and how long all the doors were wide open to let us move in, and with that, the cold as well. I am sure that next month's bill will look much different and so much less. We will talk later, I must go!"

He hung up and I cried.

And yes, next month's bill was so much lower, and since we had no gas bill on top, we could manage.

The children loved the house, and Dean made his first steps in early spring, and in the summer, was without diapers.

Sabrina found new friends and liked her teacher and the school.

It was amazing how quickly we felt at home because I think, in principle, we worked on it and wanted to.

After a year or so, I looked and found a babysitting job again, which helped a bit with paying our monthly bills.

Both parents came to introduce me to their three-year-old boy named Kevin, who looked very frail and, as I learned, was on baby food because he had a stomach problem and was also still in diapers.

"I assume you see his doctor often?" I asked.

"No," his mother answered, "Not so much anymore because he is much better and the most is over, but we should avoid dairy. And please keep him on baby food!"

"Baby food?" I asked. "So when did you see the doctor last?"

They didn't answer my question, but said instead, "Well, we don't want to risk him getting sick again and have kept him on baby food."

His wife Katy, who spoke a bit of German, interfered and told me, "Don't worry, he is doing fine."

"You see," his father continued, "We are both working again, both for Air Canada and we have to make sure that our working hours are in concert with our private life. Going often to Kevin's specialist takes time, but since he is fine now, we don't worry too much anymore."

I was very skeptical; I felt sorry for the kid but was not too keen on his parents.

I told them that I would try, and we started on the following Monday.

Little Kevin was so very scared of all of us, and it took me half a day to make him even sit down.

Dean didn't eat baby food at all anymore, and Kevin didn't like the food his parents brought for him, either, and so I gave Kevin some food that Dean had and, guess what, he ate it and liked it.

A few days later I mentioned the little change to his parents, but was told to be so very careful, even though his doctor had suggested a change. As they said, they didn't want to take the risk, and I understood why Kevin looked so very undernourished. OK, it made common sense not to go right away full blast with normal food, but slowly. He needed to eat properly.

I had the funny feeling that they were not too pleased that their son liked normal food better because baby food came in jars and, for them, jars were more convenient.

About a week later, Kevin had normal stool, and I thought it was time to train him to go to the bathroom or to the potty. He was too old to be in diapers.

I bought a second potty and made him go on it. He sat there for a while and peed, and I think he surprised himself when he saw the pee and that I was so pleased with him. I made a big fuss about it and, including little Dean, we were all happy.

He was fully trained in two weeks, but all his parents were saying was that they would bring more underwear in case he had an accident. There was no "thank you" or anything. So strange.

Well, Kevin was so meagre and thin compared to Dean; I sure had to watch that Dean never played rough with him. Dean was a year younger but sometimes took over by pushing him, yet Kevin would never defend himself. He would start crying, and Dean was often in trouble.

I babysat Kevin for a bit over a year when my mother-in-law came to visit again. We had a long weekend, and Kevin's parents picked him up a bit earlier that Friday, which was nice because I had so many things to do before Die's mom's arrival the next day.

We all were excited, especially Sabrina, who adored her grandmother. Dean didn't know her yet, but *Oma* saw him as a little baby when she came the last time to visit, and so he was just wondering who she was and if she was bringing him a present.

Later at the airport, our children, who found the airport boring, started to run around rather than wait for their grandmother to arrive. As a matter of fact, we almost missed her by looking constantly around for the kids, until Die had had enough and had a word with them.

Oma came without us seeing her coming towards us and was standing suddenly beside us when Sabrina screamed, *"Oma, my Oma Else!"* and was in no time in her arms. Dean cried because he felt left out.

We drove home and realized that Mutti looked very tired from the long flight. I guess the time difference didn't make it any easier, but after we arrived at home, she unpacked some of her suitcase and gave the children their presents. Finally, Sabrina and Dean had settled down a bit and played quietly.

Oma admired the house, and after we had our supper, she wanted to go to sleep and slept until 10 in the morning. I made her a nice breakfast and she was ready to boogie.

She played with the children a bit but wanted to go to High Park.

Since our move, High Park wasn't close by anymore, but it was nice outside and Dietmar didn't mind driving at all, so we went. After we had a lovely walk, and everybody had their ice cream, and we had gone back home and again, she couldn't get over our beautiful house. We had dinner and all took it easy.

The next day, on Monday, she was still recovering from the time change and since Dietmar took some holidays for the week we had time to relax. We both were prepared to entertain her, which was not hard because she enjoyed the kids very much and went along with our daily routine.

I mentioned Kevin and told her a bit about him, but again, she didn't mind since I would have to look after him only for four days during her stay.

She understood that for us it was a bit of extra money, and Kevin was so much better that we both couldn't think of any problems.

Prior to her visit, I asked Kevin's parents if it would be all right to take a week off and was told not to worry because they could ask Kevin's grandparents to take him for the week. But the father had to bring him on Monday and when he came with Kevin the next day, Mutti was so nice to him, too, and he didn't feel left out.

Everything went fine until Kevin's father came in the afternoon to pick him up. I dressed Kevin while his father put the payment for the previous week on the table and when I looked up, I saw small change.

"What is the change for?" I asked.

"Oh, I picked him up earlier last Friday, remember? And this is the balance I owe you, less for the two hours."

I didn't understand at first but looked at him in disbelief and was shocked. I pushed all the money, including the change towards him

and told him to keep it all and to leave our house. I almost screamed, "I am not able to babysit Kevin. I am sorry for Kevin, but I can't do it anymore. Please go! I don't need your tip!"

He protested and told me that he must find another babysitter first, but I answered, "This is not my worry any longer, please take Kevin and leave."

He left, and I never heard from them again. I was a mess after, and my mother-in-law was in dismay, she didn't understand a word; she realized that I was very upset and wanted to know what had happened. After I explained and told her the details that Lena, when I babysat Susan, never deducted a penny, that it was I who gave her back money when she offered to pay for holidays or short days. Lena needed every penny, but Kevin's parents had a very good income. So, yes, I felt used. I gave Kevin everything he needed and so much more. His parents probably would have still fed him baby food or kept him in diapers.

And after, I was very upset because I felt sorry for Kevin.

Mutti understood and took me in her arms saying, "Don't give it a thought; you did your best for this child and his father didn't appreciate it at all. Yes, I, too, feel sorry for their child."

When Die came home and heard what happened, he was pleased because he was never in agreement with me babysitting Kevin since he had the feeling that I was always so much stricter with Dean than I was with Kevin.

The visit with my mother-in-law was so nice and, for me, it was easier that I had only our kids to look after during her visit.

Dietmar again took us to many new places and *Oma* loved and enjoyed being with us.

She loved Grand Bend on Lake Huron and Suable Beach in the Bruce Peninsula. The beaches there were wonderful, and the weather helped.

We had picnics almost every day, and she enjoyed the Canadian summer; it was warm and gorgeous.

The kids adored their *Oma*, and she played so nicely with them that, again, it was a pleasure to have her with us.

But time, as always, goes fast when you have fun and before we knew it, she had to leave us.

Soon we were in our routine, and I became homesick and a bit depressed. I wished I could have seen my foster-mother, but we had no money to send her the fare, and she couldn't afford the fare either.

We lived almost two years in our house, and money was always scarce; the second mortgage was a bit much for our budget, and it would come due soon. Dietmar worked often day and night to make ends meet.

My husband, the love of my life, did everything possible to give us a good life.

He entertained the kids, and they loved him for it, and, therefore, he was always the "good guy"; he had never a strict word with them. He left that part up to me.

At Christmas of last year, Uncle Henry told us that we should send only $50 instead of the $100 for paying up our debts and should consider the $50 as a Christmas present.

Dietmar and I danced after we received the letter, and I couldn't thank him enough for the very generous present. (We made a payment right away towards the second mortgage.)

One day, Dietmar came home and told us that he had found another job at Kaylee Textiles Ltd. in Hamilton and had already had an interview. If he got the job, he would quit his old position at once with one weeks' notice prior to the weekend and would start the new job right after at the new company without losing any money.

I didn't know what hit me. I was upset because he hadn't mentioned one word about it to me until that day. It was a surprise and somehow I was in shock.

"Why?" I asked.

The answer was, "I will make more money!"

"Hamilton is far. Will you have transportation from here?"

"No, I have to take our car. We will get our shopping done on weekends for now, and after we will see how we will manage further."

And so it was. He got the job and needed a bit more money for gas. However, he liked the job very much and the increase in salary he made helped.

In July 1967, I read the newspaper and saw an advertisement for new houses in Burlington. They were about $3,000 cheaper than the

houses where we were, and the down payment was only $500. If we sold our house and moved to Burlington, which was closer to Die's work, we could make enough money to pay the second mortgage off, have lower monthly mortgage payments and could also pay Uncle Henry back. In other words, we would be out of debt.

The more I thought about it, the more excited I became about the whole idea.

That night, after we had dinner and the children were in bed, I presented my plan, and this time Dietmar was choked. He said that it was ridiculous to even think about moving.

"We haven't lived here for even two years, and you think it is good to move again? Forget it!"

We had an argument, and we both couldn't sleep.

In the morning, things looked different and at night, when he returned from work, he told me that he thought about it a lot and maybe it was a way out to reduce our debts.

"Try to find a real estate agent to find out what we could get for our house first and after we can decide."

The move to Burlington

I found an agent, and after he looked at the house, he gave me an estimate of how much money he thought he could sell our house for. It was for a better price than I guessed, but the salesman would get a percentage for his commission, and after I was not too much out with my calculation.

On the weekend, we looked at the property in Burlington and liked what we saw.

They had one house on Cindy Lane, which would be ready to move into in about a month, but again, there were other models, and we had to let them know soon because the houses were going like hotcakes.

We had our house on the market on Monday, and within two weeks it was sold. The only thing was, we had to be out of the house two weeks after closing.

Back to Burlington the next day, we bought the house we wanted and were promised we could move in on closing day of our house.

Our lawyer was not too impressed because it didn't leave him much time for the paperwork, but he promised to do his best.

When we told Uncle Henry about our plans, he understood and had no problem with it, and when we mentioned that we would be able to pay him back, he paused for a moment and then answered, "We will see."

The move went not without a bit of trouble because the new house was still surrounded by mud, but again, we managed, and as I remember, the moving company was very helpful and tried not to ruin anything.

Sabrina had a really nice room there, and Dean liked his too. It was a raised bungalow and the backyard was even nicer than the one we had in Clarkson. The only thing was, we didn't have a garage, only a carport, which Dietmar, later in spring, closed partly in. He did a very good job and some neighbours copied his design.

So, we moved again, and our family in Germany called us "gypsies." They couldn't understand because in Germany between 1945–75, houses or apartments were still few, and whoever had a place to live in, stayed put until they died.

We liked it in Burlington very much; the neighbourhood, in general, was nice, especially our next-door neighbours Gord and Joyce, who were wonderful, and it became a good friendship. (Later, we stayed in contact with them for the longest time.)

They invited us quite often to parties.

On Canada Day, the four of us went to Kitchener to a restaurant, to where Gord knew the owner and had a lot of friends as well, and I became quite tipsy.

I loved Black Russians and was mostly sober after drinking eight shots, and since Dietmar couldn't drink alcohol, the rest of us had a very a good time, we only had a little bit too much to drink.

All the guests were in a good mood and actually made bets whether I would take on another one, and Dietmar became worried and said "no" for me.

After, we stayed a bit longer until a friend of Gordy's suggested that we should have a bit to eat and invited us to his house. There, before his wife served food, I can't remember if or what we ate, he served wine, homemade wine, and after I had one glass, I must have passed out because we all suddenly were in our car and were stopped by police. The officer had one look at us all, and Dietmar had to step out of the car. It was very embarrassing, but we laughed and carried on being silly. Thanks to Dietmar, who was cool and collected, the officer wanted to let us go, but somehow was worried because he said that we should leave the windows down, otherwise Dietmar would get drunk from just breathing in what we three were breathing out.

The four of us never forgot the outing and when we talked about it, we all recalled it as a very good time and showed me respect for how much I was capable to drink. I was somehow laughing about it, but it was very embarrassing.

So yes, life was good, and we had fun.

We had by now many friends in Canada, and Germany was suddenly far away from us.

We were settled in Burlington, and it was nice because our friends Ruth and Richard moved close to us as well, just a street further into the same development.

We had a cat, our second cat (the first one, Snow, was hit by a car); it was Sabrina's cat and she looked after "Tramp" and told me that we were out of cat food, and since it was Saturday, Sabrina and I went to the pet store to get some. While I was paying for the food, Sabrina looked around and came running back to me, yelling, "Mom, you have to see the puppies they have! Come and look, they are so sweet, you have to see them. Please!"

She dragged me down the aisle, and she was right, there was this litter of beautiful little poodle puppies, two pitch black and two brown ones. It was hard not to hug them, and we both had a hard time leaving the store.

Returning back home, we found Dietmar and Dean in the backyard, like always, horsing around, but Sabrina interrupted by telling her father right away that we almost bought a puppy. She was so excited, she screamed that Dean had only heard the word "puppy" and wanted to have a look at it since he thought we had bought one. He was sad that he misunderstood and asked right away, "Why didn't you buy it?" and I answered, "Because it was expensive, and we don't need a dog at the moment."

"How come Sabrina has a cat?"

"Because she looks after the cat, and you are too young to look after a dog. Dogs are different; they need a lot of care when they are puppies."

I calmed him down and told him that I liked the puppies, too, especially the brown ones, but again, we couldn't have one in the moment, maybe later.

An hour later or so, Sabrina and Die disappeared without telling where they were going, and when I asked Dean if he knew where they were, he told me that he didn't know, either, and would look for them.

Not long after, the three came into the backyard and what did Sabrina carry in her arms? A little black bundle of fur, a black poodle puppy. I had tears in my eyes because I couldn't believe that Dietmar went with Sabrina to buy this little package of joy.

Dean danced because he knew all about it but was so proud that he had kept the secret. He had to give his father his word not to tell until the puppy was in my arms. We named her Cindy like the street we lived on. She was a good dog and was with us for eleven years when she picked up a virus from the street, became very sick and died.

Uncle Henry and Aunt Hedy, unfortunately, never saw our houses in Clarkson nor in Burlington. Both were not too well and stopped travelling, but when we sent the money we owed Uncle Henry, he sent it back and told us that it was his present to us for being so sincere and honest in handling our debts. I think to this day that he helped us to settle in Canada without regrets.

They both died, and their fortune went mainly to his niece, who returned back to Austria where she and Aunt Hedy were born.

My first job in Canada

The children grew fast. Dean was four by then and was a good boy, a bit wild, without fear of anything, I would say, like his father.

Sabrina grew up to be a typical little lady, at almost eleven and was pretty and very cute. On top of that, she was very smart and competitive in school, but compared to her brother, had no interest in sports.

She played always the 'little mother to Dean,' which he hated, and we had to watch them because they would fight, be it for toys or other possessions, but in principle, they were our pride and joy.

Both adored their father, who did anything to make them happy. He hardly ever corrected them or said a harsh word; that was my job, and conveniently he left that part up to me.

One early morning, I looked out of the front window and saw Joyce, our next-door neighbour, leaving for work. I became somehow jealous and thought, how nice it would be to go to work again, have a change of interest and make some extra money.

Our neighbour had two children, too; they were a bit older and both went full time to school already, which probably made a difference for Joyce, between staying at home or going to work again.

She told me once that she was sick and tired of staying home not being able to work, but since the children were both in school and were old enough to stay for a while by themselves, she was glad to go back to work. And as she said, she was so much happier and working was great.

That night, after the children were in bed, I talked to Dietmar about it and, at first, he was upset that I was even thinking of working again but suggested that we would need to find a babysitter for Dean. He asked, "Would it be worthwhile going back to work?"

He had a point, but somehow the prospect of getting out of the house stayed in my head.

A few weeks later, Dean played across the road, and I tried to call him. Since he didn't listen, I had to go over to get him.

The mother of his little friend came out of the house to call her boy in for lunch as well, and we said "hi" and, like neighbours do, started to talk a bit when she mentioned that she was looking for a babysitting job. Right away, I looked up and said, "And I would like to go back to work and in case I do find a job, would you babysit Dean?"

"Well, that would be great," she answered. "Let me know."

After looking into newspapers, I realized it would be probably best for me to approach an agency.

A few days later, I found one and called and, with my not-too-perfect English, explained that I had seen their advertisement and that I would be interested; but would I qualify?

The lady who answered asked me what my last job in Germany was and invited me for an interview the next evening.

Dietmar was not happy about my idea but agreed to drive me to the place and waited for my return outside, sitting in our car for almost an hour.

He was not in the best mood and asked, "What took you so long?" But after I told him the details, he cooled down.

The interview was not easy for me, yet I talked myself through it and was referred two days later to see a gentleman at the Fuller Brush Company, which was located in Burlington, not too far from where we lived.

I was scheduled for the interview the next day, early in the morning, and since Dietmar had to go to work a bit later than usual, I had the car.

The building of Fuller Brush was modern and new, and my first impression of the company was good, but I was scared and nervous that I almost wanted to return to my car.

I wasn't sure by then if I wanted to go through with it all, but I decided, if I didn't try, I would never be able to do it at all.

I went in and had to wait and again, for a while, my nerves were getting worse by the minute, but somehow, by the time I was called in, I became sure of myself and thought; *If I don't get the job I will try for another one. I will not give up!*

After about twenty minutes of being interviewed and another fifteen minutes of waiting afterwards, I had the job and was to start the following Monday. The working hours were from 9 A.M. to 4 P.M. and my salary was $300 a month plus two weeks of paid holidays. All suited me fine.

When I came home, I was very happy until Dietmar mentioned transportation. "And how will you make it to work? Is there a bus connection?"

Oh God, I didn't even think about that at all because I never believed I would get a job that quickly and answered, "No, there is no bus going in that direction and you know it. The only thing I can think of is to buy a car: I take the old car, and we buy you another car."

The next day, on Saturday, we all went shopping for a car.

We found a very reasonable used semi-automatic Volkswagen for me, and Dietmar kept the old car.

Oh, how I loved my little car; it was wonderful and so was the whole arrangement. Dean liked his babysitter, and I liked my new job. Mind you, I had much to learn because in Germany we were very much behind with how we worked. For instance, we had only one calculator for the whole office and had to do a lot manually. Here, each person had a calculator and was expected to use it and be quick. The book-keeping was principally the same but because of my language skills, I was not ready to cope with business. Talking to people was a pain. On top of all that, I had a supervisor who hated Germans and let me very often feel it too. At one time, she told me that she lost her uncle in the war and hated Germans. Another time she told me to speak English not English with a German accent. But I took it and didn't complain. I wanted to learn as much as I could from her before changing my job.

I stayed with Fuller Brush for a bit over a year and left over an argument with my supervisor.

I wanted to take my holidays together with Dietmar, but my supervisor plainly refused to give her OK. She asked me who I thought I was, and further she continued, "I have been working here for this company many years but never took more than one week at a time and, by the way, I plan to take my holidays at the same time as yours, but I certainly have seniority. So, you see, since we can't take time off at the same time, you have to take yours later and only one week, not two at once."

I was very upset about her attitude and the way she talked to me, and when I told Dietmar about it, he said, "Why don't you quit?"

Of course, I didn't want that, but I came back to her my way.

I called the same agency, which referred me to my present position, and I was lucky. They had a job for me at Niagara Chemical, in Burlington, and told me, if I were to get that job, and they believed I would, I would be much happier there than where I was, but it would be in A/C Receivable rather than in A/C Payable.

"The pay will be almost the same, but you would have a chance to advance."

Two days later, after work, I went to the interview. It was raining so badly that when I arrived there, I had no clue how to get out of my car without getting soaked. Sitting in the car for a moment, looking at the pouring rain I found a newspaper on the back seat, grabbed it, covered my hair and ran as fast as I could across to the entrance. Needless to say, I was completely soaked; but I arrived on time.

I got the job, and much later, the VP of Finance laughed when he told me that when he saw me running through the rain for my interview, he was amused and thought *that girl is dependable*. He said that this alone made him look at me and my credentials a bit closer.

He was informed prior by the agency about my knowledge and that I was bilingual in German and English (what English?) and, apparently, that was what they were looking for.

I quit my job at Fullers a week prior to my supervisor's plans to take her holidays, and went to her manager rather than talking to her, simply because I didn't want another argument with her.

She came to me after she heard about my resignation and questioned me, but all I said to her was that she should change her attitude towards Germans because, after all, when I was a kid during and after the war, I had sure suffered enough for the atrocities Hitler did during his reign.

We had our holidays as planned and, I must say, I was relieved that I didn't have to go back to Fuller Brush where my supervisor made it impossible for me to enjoy my job.

I stayed with Niagara Chemicals/FMC for seven years and during that time was promoted to credit manager. I loved my work and was loved by all my co-workers and management.

The kids grew up fast and, moneywise, we were much better off as well. As a matter of fact, we bought a VW camper but sold it not too long after because it didn't have the horsepower it needed to take even small hills and required almost a prayer to make it to the top. We replaced the VW with a little house trailer.

Dietmar was an outdoor person, and as long as he could be with his family together and had some toys, he was happy.

The children loved him, and there was never a boring time for them. He knew how to entertain them by doing all sorts of things, sometimes even stupid things, and the three of them had no fears, where I was scared often and I almost peed my pants just watching them.

He didn't smoke; he didn't drink, but he needed to be outside with his children.

We all had good times, and the good memories remain.

The children wanted a tent, as they said they wanted to sleep outside and, as Sabrina mentioned, to have more privacy, and so Dietmar went out with them to buy a tent.

At first, they were proud to have their own "house" until one rainy morning Sabrina ran out and yelled, "I can't stand it in there. Dean constantly farts, and I can't take the smell any longer. The tent stinks. Can I come into the trailer?"

Dean appeared too, laughing his head off yelling, "And you know who started first? Sabrina, but mine are better, and she couldn't take that; she always has to be the best, but she lost, ha, ha!"

We laughed, too, but a bit later when we had our breakfast, we had to stop them talking about the subject.

At night we wondered if the tent was out, and they wanted to come back into the trailer, but no, they went back to sleep in their "house," smell or not, and continued sleeping in their tent during that whole summer season.

We stayed a few summers at the same camping place on Balsam Lake and learned to know many people there who came from all over Ontario. Most of them were born in Canada, but the generation before them were all immigrants. There was never a laugh about our German accent or even a question about our heritage. For them, we were immigrants who tried hard to blend in.

One night, Dietmar had a phone call, apparently from a headhunter and was asked if he would be interested in working for a hosiery company located in Toronto.

"Toronto?" I overheard, but after Dietmar was assured that it wouldn't be at McGregor, his old company, he continued with the conversation.

They talked for at least one hour on the phone, and Dietmar agreed to have an interview.

He changed his job within two weeks and started with Dominion Hosiery for more money and without shiftwork at all.

I started a new position as well because Niagara Chemicals/FMC had sold the chemical division to Reichhold Ltd., which was located close to the airport in Toronto.

I didn't have to look for a new job because I was asked by the new company to continue to work for them. The offer was very generous, and I could keep my seniority as well.

I started at their printing equipment division, Sears, a division of Reichhold Ltd. and at first I had been hired as the assistant credit manager. However, not for long since my boss neglected his job by not acting as a manager, it seemed. He didn't stop customers from buying without paying on time. And later he was released.

The Sears division of Reichhold Ltd. dealt with printing equipment, parts and service, imported from Heidelberger Druckmaschinen Aktiengesell-schaft (AG), Germany, which later became Heidelberg Canada.

The equipment was very expensive and reliable, and customers who invested a lot of money in the equipment didn't feel they had to pay for parts and service on the terms Heidelberg offered. Needless to say, the accounts were in a mess.

I talked to Kevin, my manager, about it, but I was told that he was very busy and had no time for collection. He said, "By the way, that was the reason you were hired, and further, it is your responsibility to collect and to clean up the accounts."

I shook my head and argued that so many accounts should be on COD, even in collection but noticed that he still approved orders regardless if the accounts were overdue. He looked at me, finally, as if I had come from the moon and told me with a straight face to do my job and not to bother him any longer. "Go, and close the door behind you!"

Well, after that, I had so much that my job became overwhelming.

One day I was called by our VP of Finance and his assistant to see them.

I had never been before up to the executive section of our company and realized how plush everything was compared to our offices one floor below.

I felt out of place and wondered if I might be fired, scared to face the music. Maybe I shouldn't have criticized my boss Kevin.

I knocked at the door, and the VP answered in a friendly tone, "Come in, please." I entered (scared to be fired), but when I looked at both of them and noticed that both smiled, I became hopeful.

After the formal greeting of "How are you?" and "Sit down please," I relaxed.

They continued by coming right to the point. "How do you like your job so far?" and "We heard good things about you." And I told them straight out that the accounts were in such bad shape and that there should be a policy and procedure on how to handle overdue accounts. There was no guidance about what to do if customers were behind with their payments and whether we should continue to sell or if there should be a policy about when to put accounts on cash-on-delivery or in collections. Many accounts were out of control and, as I told them, I was at the point of giving up.

The conversation became very serious because they realized I knew what I was talking about and somehow were pleased about the open talk.

Both looked at me and said, "Don't give up. We will talk to Kevin Weber. Meanwhile, do what you can. We will let you know and will talk again soon. We will make sure that we get the matter under control."

Two months later, Kevin was gone, and I moved into his office. A dark, little room without windows, across from the computer room.

I also had the pleasure of cleaning up the mess he left behind, and I discovered that he wrote poems rather than doing his job. Again, he was a real "number," and once in a while, I wondered how he had lasted two years in his job.

In the '60s and '70s, we had these monster-sized computers, which made a lot of noise and needed people to constantly run them, and mostly women worked in there. And I had to leave my door open or I would have suffocated.

My view was not nice. My secretary had a better place; she had her desk outside my office and was sitting close to a window and often said to me, "How can you stand it in your little cubbyhole?"

Nice, but I had to get used to the view and noise, which at times was even funny because, as I mentioned, there were mostly girls working and since the computer room was surrounded by window walls and the girls often had to bend down, the view was, I guess especially for Kevin, very interesting. After all, short skirts and hot pants were in fashion, so no wonder Kevin didn't mind his office at all.

Dietmar and I worked now in the same direction but we had a problem with the arrangement: looking after the children properly. Sabrina promised to watch Dean during lunch and an hour or so until I got home, but we knew we had to make changes. We both had to drive quite a distance to work, and it simply was too far away from our children, especially in case of an emergency.

We both liked our jobs, but it was important, we had to find a solution quickly for the children.

Sabrina was doing a good job watching Dean during lunch and an hour or so until I came home, but the responsibility was too much for her.

We had to move closer to our jobs. And so, we did (again), we moved to Mississauga where we found a brand-new townhouse on Silver Creek Road. We liked the house and the fact that it was a condo, we had no worries about the outside. We had a small little backyard, enough to sit outside and even enjoy the little park we backed on to, without mowing the grass etc.

A townhouse was ideal for us, and again, we made money on the sale of our house, but this time it was not the reason to move, it was better for us getting to work and to return quickly to the children if needed.

The children didn't like to move, especially Sabrina, who by now had roots in Burlington and by moving lost her friends and was very, very sad about it.

Dean was OK with it, at his age it was not too hard yet to make new friends, but Sabrina, by then a teenager, had a big problem.

We never realized it at the time but knew later that she never was the same, she had changed and unfortunately, we lost the closeness we had with her before.

We still went camping and had good times together, but we felt a change within her.

High school was a disaster for her and made us all very upset. She couldn't find the girlfriend she wanted so desperately, a friend she could have talked to. She, I think, was lost and did things she shouldn't have done. She came into a period in her life where she thought we were wrong, and she was right. And after she turned sixteen she left us and lived her own life. It was the worst time for all of us because she was not only pretty but was a very smart, intelligent girl, and we couldn't figure out why she would do this to herself. Or to us. She gave up her family for a strange world.

For Dietmar and myself it was a very sad time, we often couldn't sleep and cried or argued. Yes, we could never overcome our grief.

Her brother missed her as well, he too, became sad about the situation but was too young to hang on. Yes, he often tried to find her and lost her and found her again and later, gave up.

Our chalet in Sugarbush

We sold the trailer because I was tired of camping, it was a bit much for me to come home from work, pack and prepare for the weekend and two days later, return home, unpack and so on.

Die understood but was absolutely lost and suggested that we look for a cottage or something where he and Dean could still have their outside fun, and I didn't have to make sure that everybody was entertained.

We looked at cottages, and I didn't like any of them because it was cottage life that I couldn't see enjoying. I saw myself cleaning and cooking and cleaning again because I had already made myself sick of the camper, where I changed the sheets every time every weekend we came or left the trailer.

One day sitting in our dentist's office, looking through magazines, I saw an advertisement for chalets in Horseshoe Valley, not far from a resort and lots of skiing, located north of Barrie. Somehow it sounded very intriguing. I ripped out the page and showed it to Die, who was all for it and after we looked, we found a chalet.

I must say, we had a wonderful time and loved our chalet, and later we certainly never forgot all the fun we had there.

I continue to stay in contact with the neighbours we became close to during the eight years we owned the beautiful property.

Unfortunately, we had to sell it because we simply couldn't afford the high interest rates at the time we had to renew our mortgage.

Again, we made a gain on the sale, which allowed us to buy property not far away from the so-loved haven.

Two years later we build a beautiful house there and after we sold our townhouse in Mississauga we rented an apartment for a while before we moved into our dream house permanently.

We travelled for ten years back and forth to work to Toronto until we retired, first Dietmar in May, then me in September of 1998.

Dietmar enjoyed retirement right away. But I missed my job for at least a year. When people asked me why, I answered, "Because I miss the stress and the people."

I loved that job because it was challenging. The sales department sold the equipment, parts and labour, and I had to make sure that the customers paid for all these purchases on time. There were many challenges with both, the customers and the sales department. And there were legal matters, everything had to be correct, and many situations had to be handled very diplomatically. Yes, I missed this job, my colleges, the working environment, and the stress. In all the twenty-three years I worked at Heidelberg Canada, I never got tired of my work.

Epilogue

Time went by, but I must say after we received our citizenship in 1967, we never looked back and had no regrets that we left our homeland. It is nice to visit Germany, but home is Canada now.

During November of 1989, the Berlin Wall came down. We were absolutely beside ourselves, danced in our kitchen and celebrated the wonderful news by inviting all our German friends for a dinner party "Berliner Style." It was so much fun, and we were able to close the chapter because, after all, the wall was the reason we immigrated to Canada in the first place.

Sabrina came back home for a while, married and gave us two wonderful grandsons and Dean, who loved the chalet tremendously and remembers the good times we had there, found his love too, got married, and they, too, gave us two boys.

We lived in the house on Horseshoe Valley Road for twenty-eight years, but one year after Dietmar my love, passed away in June 2014 I had to sell, with a very sad and heavy heart, our home. I sadly realized it became too much for me to look after both, the beautiful property with the now much too big house.

Dietmar still had seen three of our great-grandchildren, and I feel so blessed with our two children, four grandchildren and now five great-grandchildren, where the youngest carries our last name, the third generation in Canada.

So, as you learned from reading the story, our family settled in Canada and we are very proud to be Canadians.

As I mentioned at the beginning of the book, I and many other people question our immigration laws because we realize that those who came so much earlier established this country to have a better life by simply working hard and without any expectation of receiving help from anybody.

And by all means, my story is not outstanding because so many people could tell similar stories. It is not an outstanding story because we, like prior generations, didn't have to turn the soil, plant and hunt to have food and warmth or build a shelter to survive brutal winters without any necessities.

And compared to that, later generations had it easy, but what we all should realize now and hopefully have in common is, that Canada gave us the opportunity. We worked, integrated, and settled in Canada where nobody is singled out and has the same rights.

I don't take Canada for granted, and rather I'm thankful to Canada that it opened the door for my family, and gave us the freedom to accelerate. And I hope that the future for all others who came or will come to Canada will share my thoughts and will flourish as well.

Manufactured by Amazon.ca
Bolton, ON

29262160R00092